Mel Bay Presents

Mastering the Gu[itar] 2A

MW00911952

A COMPREHENSIVE METHOD FOR TODAY'S GUITARIST!

By William Bay &
Mike Christiansen

CONTENTS

Zone I **2**
How to Practice **3**
Key of C **4**
Key of C/Closed Position 4
C Scale/Closed Position 4
C Scale/Closed Position/ Extended Range 4
Velocity Study #1 4
Velocity Study #2 5
Velocity Study #3 5
Velocity Study #4 5
Velocity Study #5 5
Etudes 6
Brandywine Hornpipe 6
Ragtime Reel 6
Logan Shuffle 6
Trumpet Air 7
Copley Two Step 7
Dauphine Strut 7
Got It 8
In Motion 8
Flatpick Arps 8
Two-Octave C Scale 9
Casa Loma Stomp 9
Castawissa Gavotte 9
Missouri Mud 10
The Entertainer 10
The Trill 11
Sheep May Safely Graze 11
Air from *Suite #3* 11
Never Too Late 12
Stone's Rag 13
Etude 14
Cookin' 15
Driving Rock 15
Soppin'the Gravy 16
Lost Indian 16
Study 17
Sight Reading 18
Springtime in Dubuque 18
Basic Improvisation 19
Basic Chords and Arpeggios in C 19
Basic Arpeggios 19
Passing Tones 19
Passing Tone Apeggio Study #1 19
Passing Tone Study #2 20
Passing Tone Study #3 20
Rhythmic Variation Study #1 20
Rhythmic Variation Study #2 21
Fingerstyle Etude #1 21
Fingerstyle Etude #2 21
Etude 22
Chords in the Key of C 23
Chord Progressions in C 25
Chord Studies in C 27
C Progression in Arpeggio Form 27
Prelude in C Major 28
Recife 32
Summer Afternoon 32
D.C. al Coda Review 33
Fortaleza 33
For Maya 33
For the New One 34
Blues in C 35
Turnarounds in C 35
Losin' You 36
Licks/Fills/Breaks in C 37
Groovin' 38
Bass Runs 38
Mama Don't 'low 42
Key of G **43**
Key of G/Closed Position 43
G Scale/Closed Position 43
G Scale/Closed Position/ Extended Range 43
G Scale Velocity #1 43
G Scale Velocity #2 44
G Scale Velocity #3 44
G Scale Velocity #4 44
National Lancer's Hornpipe 45
Witch of the Wave Reel 45
Days of 'Lang Syne 45
Sweet Lillie 46
Havana Taxi 46
Bouree 47
Pretty Saro 48
9/8 Time 48
Barney's Goat 48
Silver Bell 49
Miss McCloud's Reel 49
Summer Serenade 50
Tombigbee River 51
Prospect 51
Sinfonia from *Cantata No. 156* 52
Leather Britches 53
Bop City 53
Steep Canyon Rag 54
Basic Improvisation in G 55
Basic Chords and Arpeggios in the Key of G 55
Basic Arpeggios 55
Passing Tone Arpeggio Study #1 55
Passing Tone Study #2 55
Passing Tone Study #3 56
Rhythmic Variation Study #1 56
Rhythmic Variation Study #2 56
Rhythmic Variation Study #3 56
Jesu, Joy of Man's Desiring 57
Green Fields of America 59
Gladiator Reel 59
Pacific Blues 59
Menuett (Duet) 60
Groove Time 61
Breezin' 61
Riff for Clifford 61
Theme for Bird 62
Blue Vibes 62
"To Carlos" 62
Black and White Rag 63
Chords in the Key of G 64
G (I), C (IV), Am (ii), Em (vi), & Embellishments of G, C, Am, & Em 64
Chord Progressions in G 65
Chord Studies in G 66
Little Chorale 67
Fingerstyle Etude 67
Spring Water 68
Smooth Change 68
Fifth Avenue Swing 69
Op. 100 No. 2 70
No Goodbyes 71
Blues in G 72
Turnarounds in G 73
Mama's Blues 74
Gee Bop Blues 76
Licks/Fills/Breaks in G 77
Good Times 78
Principles of Memorization 78
Minor Pentatonic Scale (Sixth-String Root) 79
St. Louis Shuffle 80
Midnight Stroll 82
Minor Pentatonic Scale (Fifth-String Root) 84
Drive Me Away 84
Can't Do That 85
Key of D **86**
Key of D/Closed Position 86
Velocity Study #1 86
Velocity Study #2 86
Velocity Study #3 87
D Scale/Extended Range 87
Velocity Study #4 87
Extended Range Etude 87
Bonaparte Crossing the Rhine 88
Back Manner Tune 88
An Comhra Donn 89
St. Clair's Hornpipe 89
Goin' Home Blues 90
Pepe's Visit 90
Star of Bethlehem 91
Bennett's Favorite Reel 91
Fugue in D 92
Ivy Leaf Reel 93
St. Anne's Reel 93
Etude #11 94
Buttermilk Jig 94
Neapolitan Threshers 95
Whiskey Before Breakfast 95
Sauget Strut 95
Notes on the Second String 96
Second String Study #1 96
Second String Study #2 96
Basic Improvisation in D 97
Basic Chords and Arpeggios in D 97
Basic Arpeggios 97
Passing Tone Study #1 97
Passing Tone Study #2 97
Passing Tone Study #3 98
Rhythmic Variation Study #1 98
Rhythmic Variation Study #2 98
Rhythmic Variation Study #3 98
Autumn Duet from *The Four Seasons* 99
"D" Blues 101
Hornpipe from *Water Music* (Theme/Duet)- 3/2 Time 102
Notes on the Third String 104
Third String Study #1 104
Third String Study #2 104
Chords in the Key of D 105
D (I), Em (ii), G (IV), Bm (vi), & Embellishments of D, Em, G, & Bm 105
Chord Exercises in D 106
Chord Studies in D 107
Evening Shade 107
Meditation 108
Hazy Afternoon 108
Mother Has Come With Her Beautiful Song 109
Fair Flower of Northumberland 109
Swingin' on a Cloud 110
Lovely Love 111
Theme from 'Winter' (Duet from *The Four Seasons*) 112
Notes on the Fourth String 114
Fourth String Study #1 114
D String Boogie 114
Arkansas Traveler 115
Jock O' Hazeldean 116
Cottonwood Samba 117
Rondo 118
Saltarello 119
Allegro 120
Canary Jig 122
Study in D 123
Gavotte I from *Cello Suite #6* 124
Clair de Lune 125
Blues in D 128
Turnarounds in D 128
Atlantic Blues 129
Licks/Fills/Breaks in D 130
Louisiana Connection 131
Principles of Successful Performance 132
Moveable Power Chords 133
Rock Comping 136
12/8 Time 139
She's Gone Away 139
Key of B Minor **140**
The Natural B Minor Scale 140
Velocity Study 140
The B Harmonic Minor Scale 140
Velocity Study 140
Harvest Moon Strathspey 141
Brighton Beach 141
Low Rider 141
Caliente 141
Alastair's Lament 142
Avenging and Bright 142
Luckie Bawdins' Reel 142
Deco Dance 143
Last Tango in Skokie 143
North Sea 144
Puttin' on the Glitz 144
Etude 145
Soaring 147
Marziale 148
Notes on the Fifth String 150
"A" Drive 150
"A" Boogie 150
B Minor Swing 151
Remembrance 151
Luna Noche 151
Basic Improvisation in Bm 152
Basic Chords and Arpeggios in Bm 152
Basic Arpeggios 152
Passing Tone Study #1 152
Passing Tone Study #2 152
Passing Tone Study #3 153
Rhythmic Variation study #1 153
Rhythmic Variation study #2 153
Rhythmic Variation study #3 153
Preludio 154
Jezebel Carol 156
Noël Nouvelet 156
Minuet 157
Northumbrian Dance 157
Hired Hands 158
Notes on the Sixth String 159
Walkin' Jazz 159
Funky Sixth 159
Bouree from *Suite #2* 160
Embarcadero 161
Chords in the Key of B Minor 162
Bm (I), D (iii), Em (iv), G (VI), & Embellishments of Bm, D, Em & G 162
Chord Studies in B Minor 165
B Minor Etude #1 165
B Minor Etude #2 166
El Brujo 167
Bad Vibes 167
Lagoa Azul 168
Smoothie 168
Romance of Spain 169
Jungle Fever 171
Visions of Madrid 172
B Minor Waltz 173
Etude 174
Study in Bm 175
Prelude 177
Blues in B Minor 179
Got the Time 180
Licks/Fills/Breaks in B Minor 181
Somethin' for Nothiin' 183

Available in 2002 to supplement this series:

Jazz Theory Handbook — book/CD set
Guitar Workbook/Learning Guitar Fingerboard Theory — book
Mastering the Guitar Class Method/Elementary to 8th Grade Level — book & 2-CD set
Mastering the Guitar Class Method/Beginning-9th Grade and Higher — book & 2-CD set
Mastering the Guitar/Teacher's Supplement (Level 1 & 2) — books
Mastering the Guitar Class Method (Levels 1 & 2) — books & CDs
Mastering the Guitar Lesson Plans (Levels 1 & 2) — books
Mastering the Guitar Ensembles (Levels 1 & 2) — books
Mastering the Guitar Theory Workbook/Test Booklet (Levels 1 & 2) — books
Mastering the Guitar/Level 2 — CD set
Stringing the Guitar Chart — chart

1 2 3 4 5 6 7 8 9 0

© 1998 BY MEL BAY PUBLICATIONS, INC., PACIFIC, MO 63069.
ALL RIGHTS RESERVED. INTERNATIONAL COPYRIGHT SECURED. B.M.I. MADE AND PRINTED IN U.S.A.
Visit us on the Web at www.melbay.com — E-mail us at email@melbay.com

Basics

Zone I

In Zone I, the 1st Finger of the Left Hand will always be between the First and Third frets.

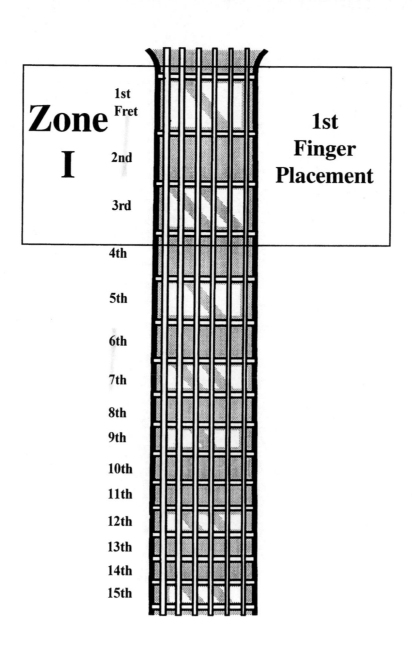

How to Practice

Practicing correctly can make a world of difference in the quality of your playing and the amount of time it takes to learn to play the guitar. Like learning a piece of music, the art of practicing can also be learned. Written below are some tips, which if followed, will make you a better guitarist and musician.

1. Practice with a goal in mind. To achieve the most from your practicing, you should set *attainable* goals. Organize these goals in such a way that you don't overwhelm yourself. Not only are you learning to play the guitar, but you are also learning patience. Progress one step at a time, being careful not to expect too much of yourself. Set short goals first, such as mastering a difficult two-measure rhythm. Then, set long goals, such as memorizing an entire piece of music. Write down your goals. It will help if you give yourself an assignment. Know your limitations, but push yourself. Expand your horizons to new levels.

2. Have a set time to practice. Generally, it is easier to establish the habit of practicing if it is done at the same time each day or night.

3. Organize your practice time. It may be helpful to write a list of goals to be accomplished during the practice time. The items on the list may change somewhat as progress is made on the music.

4. Practice in a comfortable environment. The place in which the practicing is done should have a comfortable temperature, a good, lively sound, good lighting, and be relatively free from interruptions.

Also, make sure the necessary tools such as picks, music, metronome, music stand, pencil and etc. are available.

5. Practice new music in segments. The music can be learned and memorized in a much shorter length of time if rather than going over and over the entire piece from beginning to end, the music is practiced in small sections (possibly one or two measures) at a time. Start at the beginning of the music and play one or two measures. Play the music slowly using the correct fingerings and rhythms. After that portion comes together, practice the next one or two measures. Then, play the piece from the beginning to that point. Repeat the process for the next one to two measures.

6. Isolate problem areas. In most pieces there will be trouble spots. These are small areas in the music which are more difficult to play. Locate those areas and practice them repeatedly. Then, play the music before and through the difficult portion. If you try to polish a difficult section by playing the entire piece from beginning to end, you are wasting valuable time. You don't need to spend as much time on the easier parts of a piece.

7. Have a performance goal. Even from the beginning, with a new piece of music, practice in such a way as to prepare the piece for a performance. Plan on the performance being the goal. This will help to put purpose into practicing.

8. Don't practice mistakes. A professional won't accept mistakes. If mistakes happen, correct them, rather than practicing them over and over. Listen closely to the music. Train your fingers to play the right notes!

9. Practice mentally, then physically. Without the guitar, envision yourself fingering and playing the music. See the notes. Imagine how the music should sound. Then, play the music. Sing or hum the melody.

10. Avoid boredom. Have some fun. Don't let the new music consume the practice time. Play something familiar and comfortable.

11. Use the "sandwich method" of practicing. The sandwich method refers to layering the material being practiced. Begin each practice session with older familiar and comfortable music. This could be done as part of the warm-up portion of the practice session which could also include scales and chord studies. Next, focus on new material. Finally, before the practice session is over, play older, familiar music once again. Ending the practice time on a positive note will be healthy both physically and psychologically.

12. Develop concentration. Be patient. Focus your attention on the challenges in the music. Think back on advice from your teacher and try to imagine you are the teacher. What advice would you give yourself for improving?

13. Be positive and "up." Think of the rewards which will be yours after you have mastered the music. Rather than always looking ahead at what has to be done, occasionally look back and see how far you have come. Once you see you have been reaching goals, it will help build your confidence and your practicing will be self-motivated.

14. Stick with it. Meet the challenge presented by learning new skills and music. If the going gets tough, isolate problem spots and solve them piece by piece. Remember, nothing which is of lasting value comes without work and dedication.

15. Record your practicing. It may be helpful to record practice sessions and listen for mistakes and areas which need improvement. While this might be a bit hard to digest at first, ultimately it will make you a better musician.

16. Build security. Successful practicing develops confidence. Although perfection is never guaranteed, it's much better to plan to practice until the piece is perfected than to rely on luck.

Far fewer people suffer from lack of talent than from lack of dedication, study, and preparation. If you prepare...you will play.

Key of C/Closed Position

One of the foundational building blocks in moving toward advanced guitar performance is the ability to play music in any key in various locations on up the guitar fingerboard. We have previously learned the Key of C/Open or First Position. We will now learn to play every note in the Key of C in our first closed position. By **closed position,** we mean playing every note as a fingered note...no open strings.

C Scale/Closed Position

This location of the C Scale is traditionally called **2nd position** because **the first finger of the left hand** is on the **2nd fret.**

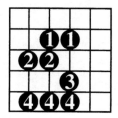

C Scale/Closed Position/Extended Range

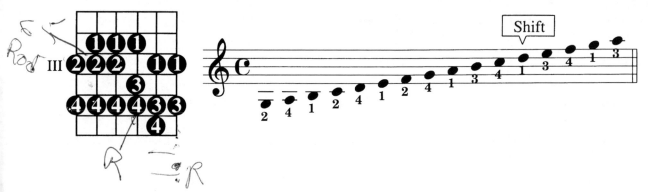

Velocity Study #1

Velocity Study #2

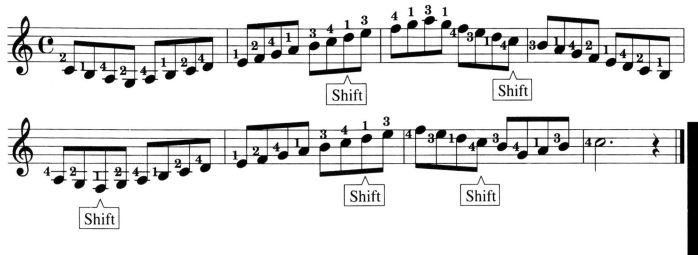

Velocity Study #3

Velocity Study #4

Velocity Study #5

Etudes

Brandywine Hornpipe

Flatpick Solo
Allegretto ♩ = 76

CD #1
Track #1

WB

Ragtime Reel

Flatpick Solo
♩ = 144

CD #1
Track #2

WB

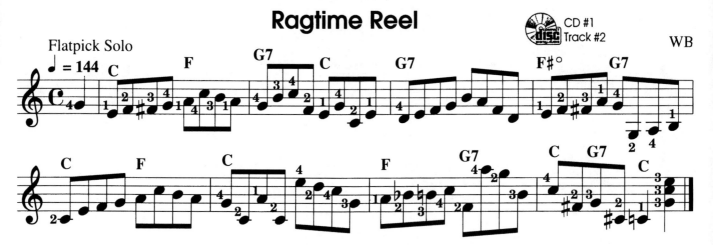

Logan Shuffle

Flatpick Solo
Swing feeling ♩ = 152

CD #1
Track #3

WB

Trumpet Air

WB
Jeremiah Clarke

CD #1
Track #4

Flatpick Solo
Stately, triumphant ♩ = 100

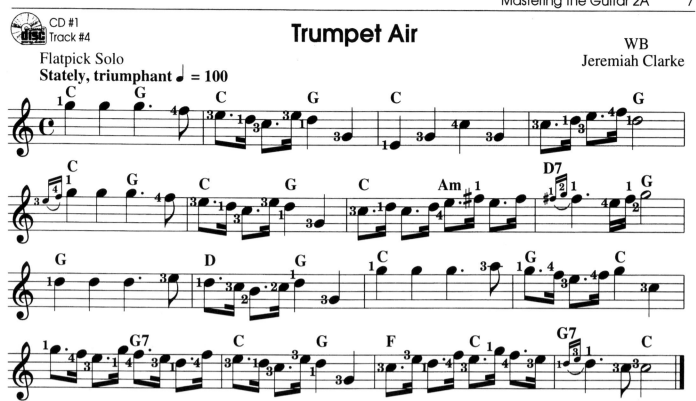

CD #1
Track #5

Copley Two Step

WB

Flatpick Solo
Swing feeling ♩ = 138

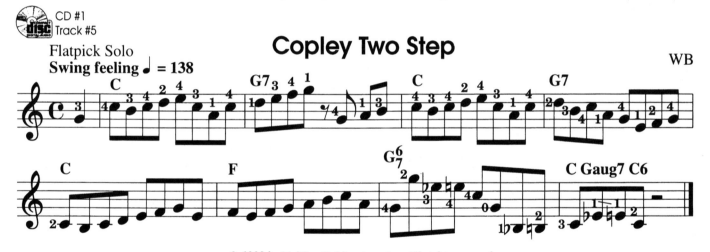

CD #1
Track #6

Dauphine Strut

WB

Flatpick Solo
Jazz waltz ♩ = 152

Key of C

Got It

Flatpick Solo

♩ = 102

CD #1
Track #7

MC

In Motion

Flatpick Solo

♩ = 76

CD #1
Track #8

MC

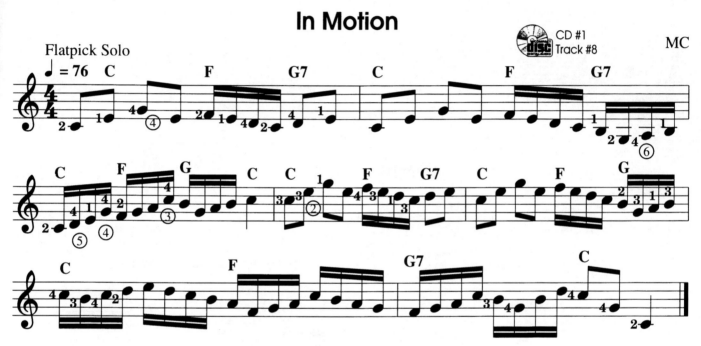

Flatpick Arps

Flatpick Solo

♩ = 102

CD #1
Track #9

MC

Key of C

Two-Octave C Scale

Note that the left hand shifts twice: once on the D, and again on the high A.

Casa Loma Stomp

CD #1
Track #10

Flatpick Solo
Swing feeling ♩ = 144

Catawissa Gavotte

CD #1
Track #11

Flatpick Solo

♩ = 100

Key of C

CD #1
Track #12

Missouri Mud

WB
Fiddle Tune

Flatpick Solo

The Entertainer

WB
Scott Joplin

Flatpick Solo

Moderate, ragtime feeling ♩ = 126

Key of C

The Trill

The **trill** is a rapid succession of notes either 1/2 step (one fret) or one whole step (two frets) apart. It uses rapid hammer-ons and pull-offs.

Sheep May Safely Graze

The following piece uses a **trill** on the second to last measure. Trills were used often in the Baroque music period. This trill should be a full step, from A to B.

arr. © 1998 by Mel Bay Publications, Inc. All rights reserved.

Air

(From *Suite #3*)

On this beautiful, well-known air by J.S. Bach, strive for clarity of tone, good vibrato, and expressive, lyrical interpretation.

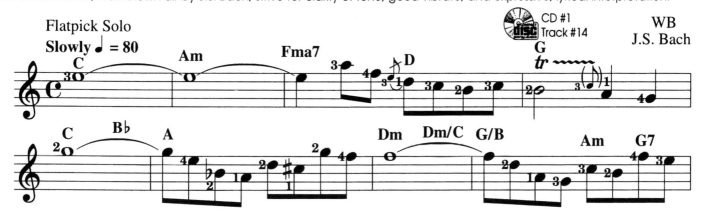

arr. © 1998 by Mel Bay Publications, Inc. All rights reserved.

Key of C

Never Too Late

CD #1
Track #15

Flatpick Solo

MC

Fine Finish here after repeating

Stone's Rag

CD #1
Track #16

WB
American Rag

Flatpick Solo
Swing feeling ♩ = 160

Etude

CD #1
Track #17

WB
Wohlfahrt

Flatpick Solo
Allegro moderato ♩ = 120

Key of C

Cookin'

CD #1
Track #18

WB

Key of C

Driving Rock

CD #1
Track #19

WB

Soppin' the Gravy

Flatpick Solo
Swing, ragtime feeling ♩ = 80

CD #1
Track #20   WB   Fiddle Tune

Key of C

Lost Indian

CD #1
Track #21   WB
American Fiddle Tune

Flatpick Solo
Lively tempo ♩ = 88

Study

The following is a famous guitar technique study. It may be played with a pick or with the fingers. In its original form it was written in open position. Here we play primarily with closed-position fingering.

CD #1
Track #22

WB
Carcassi

Flatpick Solo

$\frac{1}{2} = 60$

Key of C

Key of C

Sight Reading

When playing the guitar, it is easy to get in the habit of playing by familiar finger patterns or by familiar melodic patterns. It is important to practice sight reading to teach our fingers and ears to play what is written without falling into assumptions that can lead to the wrong note. The following study should be played slowly at first. It is atonal so as to provide a challenge to your fingers and ears.

CD #1
Track #23

Springtime in Dubuque

WB

Flatpick Solo
Allegro, rhythmically ♩ = 138

Basic Improvisation

Improvisation is an essential element of all forms of contemporary music. When studying the subject of improvising, one can get quite complex, learning various scales, modes, chord progressions, substitutions, etc. We are going to keep it simple and workable. The basic premise we will explore will be to: (1) learn the basic chord progressions for each key in arpeggio form; (2) add passing tones to that chord progressions in sequential studies; and (3) vary the arpeggio rhythmically. The end result is to train your ear and hands to hear and play variations on given chords and to work out, on your own, phrases that sound good.

Basic Chords & Arpeggios in C

(The Roman numeral denotes the degree in the C scale. Thus, F is IV because in the C scale, F is the 4th note.)

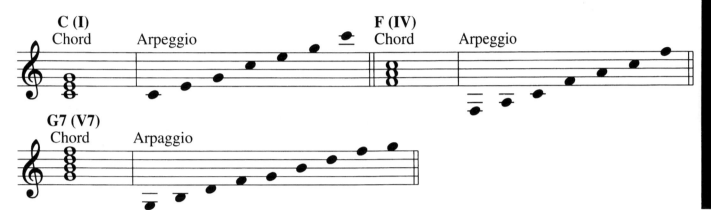

Chords/Arpeggios

Play the following studies with a jazz or swing feeling.

Basic Arpeggios

WB

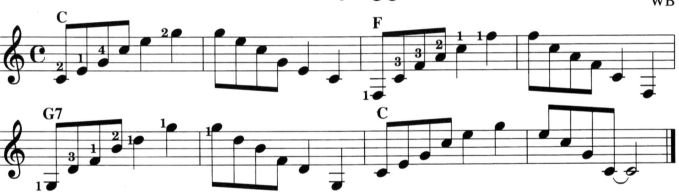

Passing Tones

Passing Tones are non-chordal notes that "ease" us into the next chordal tone.

Passing Tone Arpeggio Study #1

WB

Swing feeling

Passing Tone Study #2

WB

Passing Tone Study #3

WB

Rhythmic Variation Study #1

Here are examples of how you can vary the rhythm and melodic notes to make your own melodies.

WB

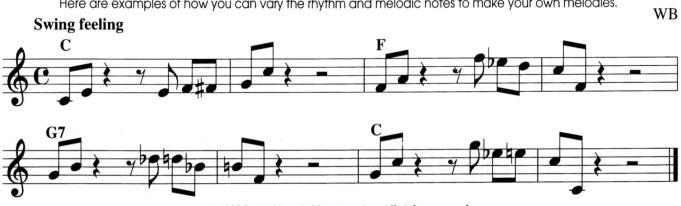

Rhythmic Variation Study #2

WB

Now try to make up your own phrases on each chord, using passing tones and varying the order of notes! Make up as many as you can. Do this exercise each day in order to train your hands and ears for improvisation!

Fingerstyle Etude #1

CD #1
Track #24

Fingerstyle Etude #2

CD #1
Track #25

MC

Fingerstyle Solos in C

Etude

This wonderful study by the 19th-Century Italian guitarist Luigi Mozzani uses **closed** and **open positions** in the **key of C.** It is a beautifully lyrical piece and can be played with a pick or fingers. It uses some left-hand stretches which may seem difficult at first (note the first four notes in measure 5). Listen carefully to the beautiful yet inventive way the composer weaves the harmonic sequences.

CD #1
Track #26

WB
Mozzani

(Strum chord
with thumb)

Drawn on the diagrams below are the chords in the key of C. The basic chords are drawn first and followed by alternate fingerings and embellishments of the chords. Embellished chords are those which have notes added to the basic chord to give color and make the chord sound more interesting. The Roman numerals in parentheses next to each chord name indicate each chord's placement (assignment) in the key. The Roman numerals to the right of some of the diagrams indicate fret number.

Occasionally chords have a slash in the name...such as G/B. These are chords over bass notes. The letter on the left indicates the basic chord and the letter on the right indicates which note is to be played as the lowest note in the chord. For example, G/B would indicate a G chord with a B note in the bass.

Learn the basic chord fingerings first and then practice the other chords.

Chords in the Key of C

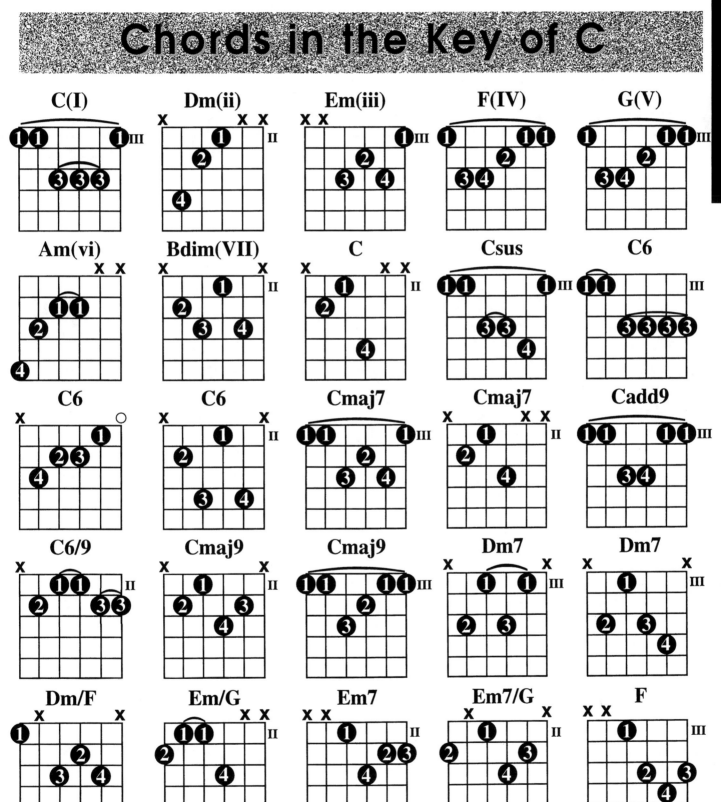

Chord in the Key of C Cont.

Chords in the Key of C

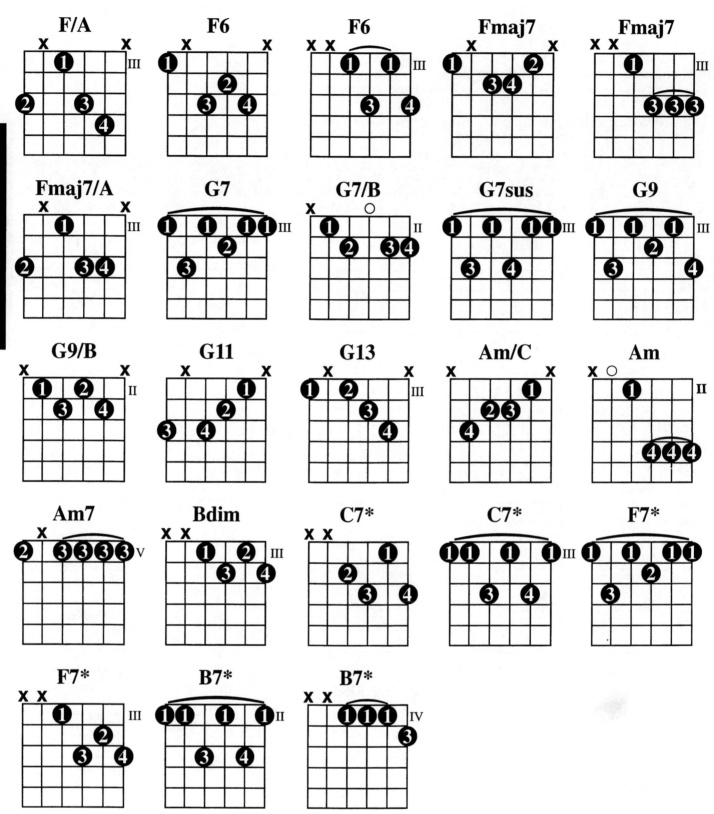

*These chords are not in the key of C, but they are commonly used when playing pieces (such as the blues) in C.

Chord Progressions in C

Practice the following chord progressions in the **key of C.** Use the strum or fingerpick pattern which is written in the first one or two measures to play each measure of the exercise. Use basic fingerings first and then try other forms of the chords.

Chords in the Key of C

Chord Studies in C

The following exercise is to be played with a pick. Because it is an arpeggio exercise, whenever possible let the notes ring.

C Progression in Arpeggio Form

CD #1
Track #27

Prelude in C Major
(From *The Well Tempered Clavier*)

This is a famous lyrical piece of music. The French composer Gounod wrote his famous setting of *Ave Maria* based on this Prelude. It may be played with a pick or fingers. Take it slowly, learning two measures at a time. Strive for smoothness, beauty of tone, and sustain on the notes.

WB
J.S. Bach

Flatpick or Fingerstyle

Largo ♩ = 58

Key of C

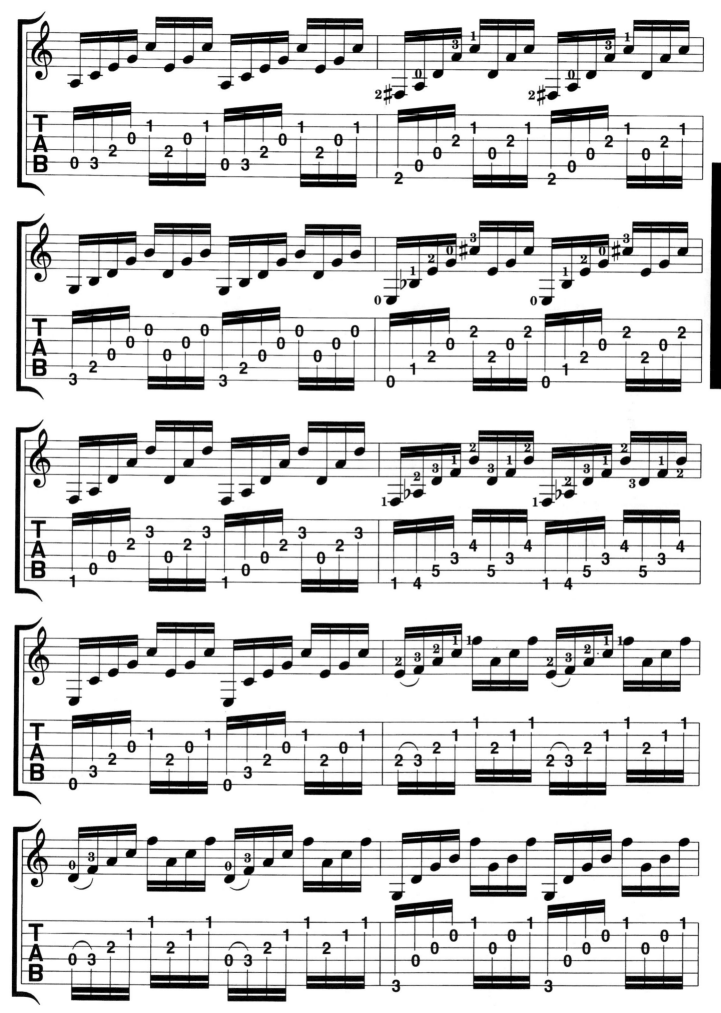

Key of C

Key of C

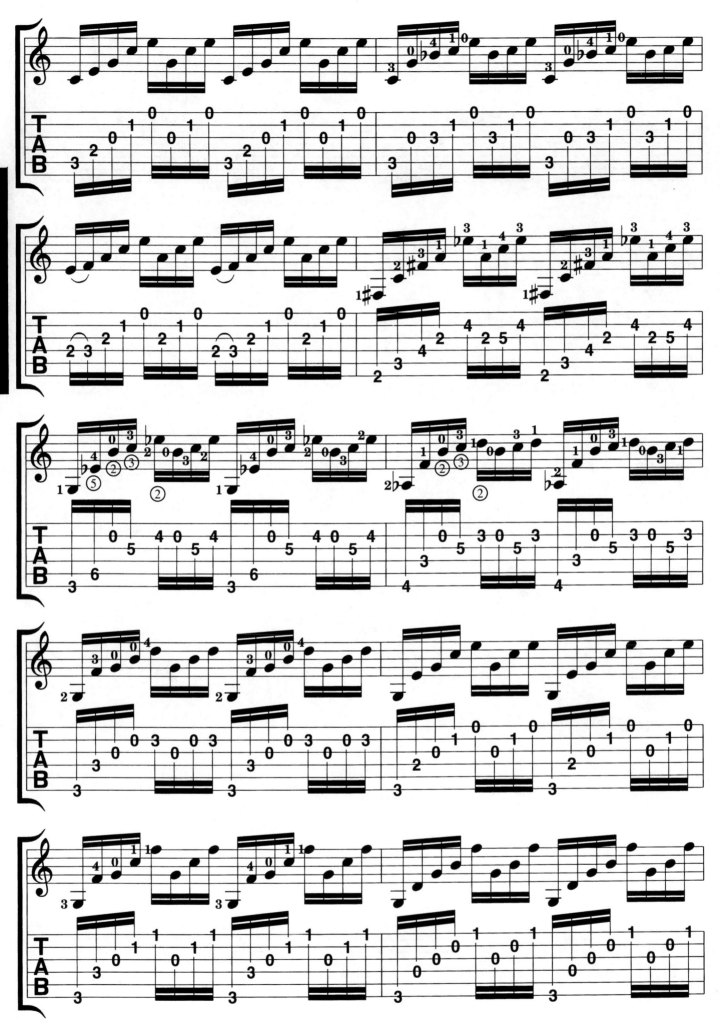

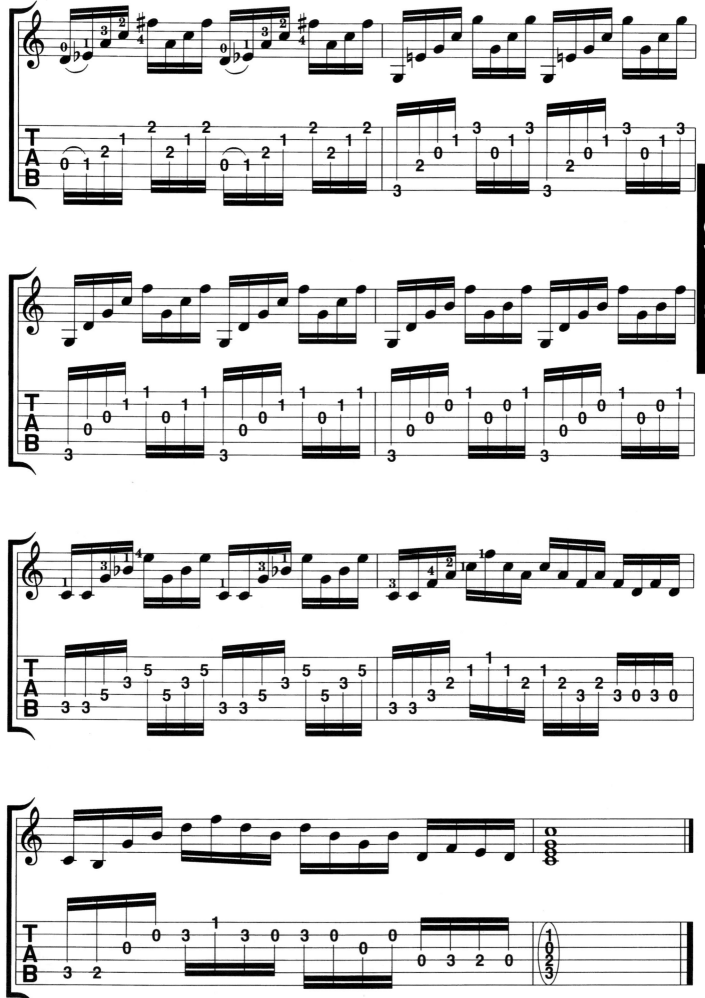

Key of C

Recife

Fingerstyle Solo
Bossa nova ♩ = 126

CD #1
Track #28

WB

Summer Afternoon

Fingerstyle Solo
♩ = 126

CD #1
Track #29

MC

D.C. al Coda Review

Remember, when you see the marking **D.C. al Coda**, go back to the beginning and play until you see the coda sign (⊕). When you reach the coda sign, skip down to the second coda sign or the ending.

Fortaleza

CD #1 Track #30   WB

For Maya

CD #1 Track #31   MC

Key of C

For the New One

CD #1
Track #32

Written below are two blues progressions in the key of C. The first is a basic progression and the second is a variation.

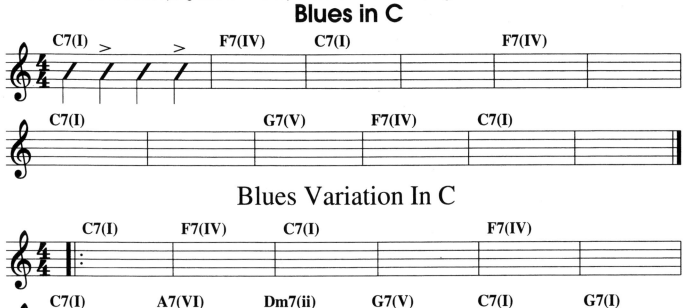

Turnarounds in C

A **turnaround** is a series of notes and/or chords which are played in the last one or two measures of the blues progression. It signals that the progression is going to be repeated or turned around. A turnaround introduces the first measure. Turnarounds may also be used as introductions. Turnarounds are an essential part of the blues. Early blues guitarists had their favorite turnarounds, many of which are still popular and used today.

Written below are many of the more popular turnarounds which may be used in the key of C. They can be used in any blues progression or song in the key of C.

The following piece is a blues in the **key of C** and contains turnarounds at the end and in the introduction. The turnarounds have been boxed so they can be easily seen.

Losin' You

CD #1
Track #33

MC

Licks/Fills/Breaks in C

Licks are a series of notes and/or chords which have a "catchy" sound. Licks are sometimes referred to as **fills** or **breaks.** They are often repeated over and over in a solo. They are also used to fill in the gaps in a vocal piece where the vocalist stops singing or in a solo when there is a gap in the melody.

Written below are some common licks and fills for the key of C.

The following piece is a flatpick solo in the **key of C** which contains licks. The licks have been boxed so they can be easily seen.

Groovin'

CD #1
Track #34

MC

Bass Runs

The following **bass runs** are used to connect two chords together. Those written in standard notation and tablature can be played with the fingers, but will probably work best with a pick. Those bass runs written in tablature only work best if played with the fingers.

These bass runs will add color and make accompaniments more interesting. Practice each bass run as written, then apply them to any music you may have.

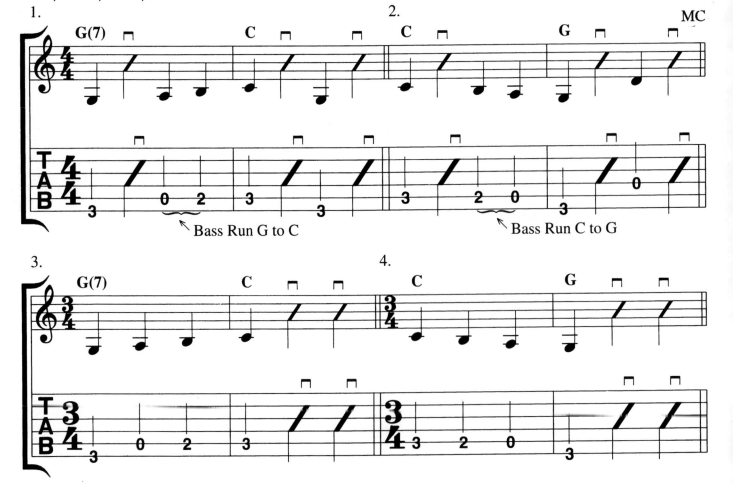

Bass Runs

Bass Runs

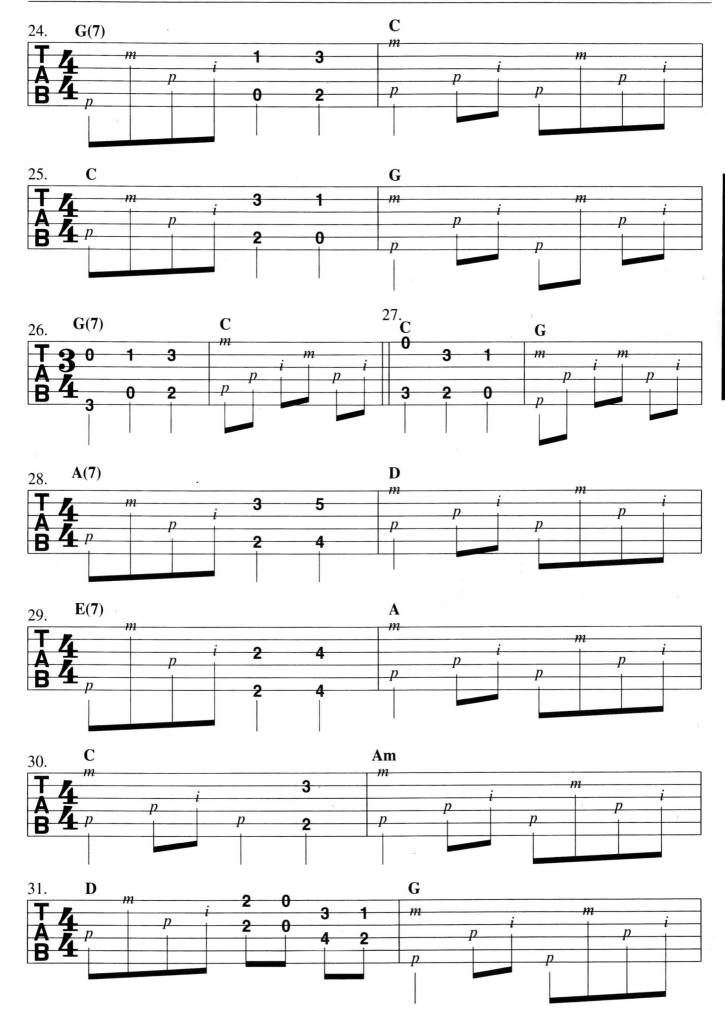

Bass Runs

The following song shows how bass runs can be used in the accompaniment. The melody is written on top and the guitar accompaniment on the bottom. In order to easily see, the bass runs have been underlined.

Mama Don't 'low

CD #1
Track #35

MC
Traditional

Bass Runs

Key of G/Closed Position

We will now learn to play the **key of G** in Zone 1/Closed Position. This means that all notes will be fingered – no open-string notes. The scale lies in what is traditionally called **2nd Position** because the **1st finger of the left hand** is on the **2nd fret.**

G Scale/Closed Position

G Scale/Closed Position/Extended Range

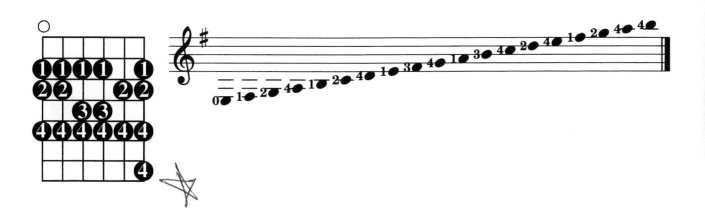

G Scale Velocity Study #1

WB

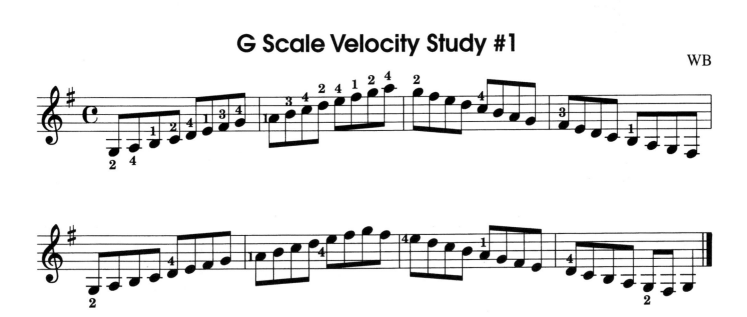

G Scale Velocity Study #2

G Scale Velocity Study #3

G Scale Velocity Study #4

Key of G

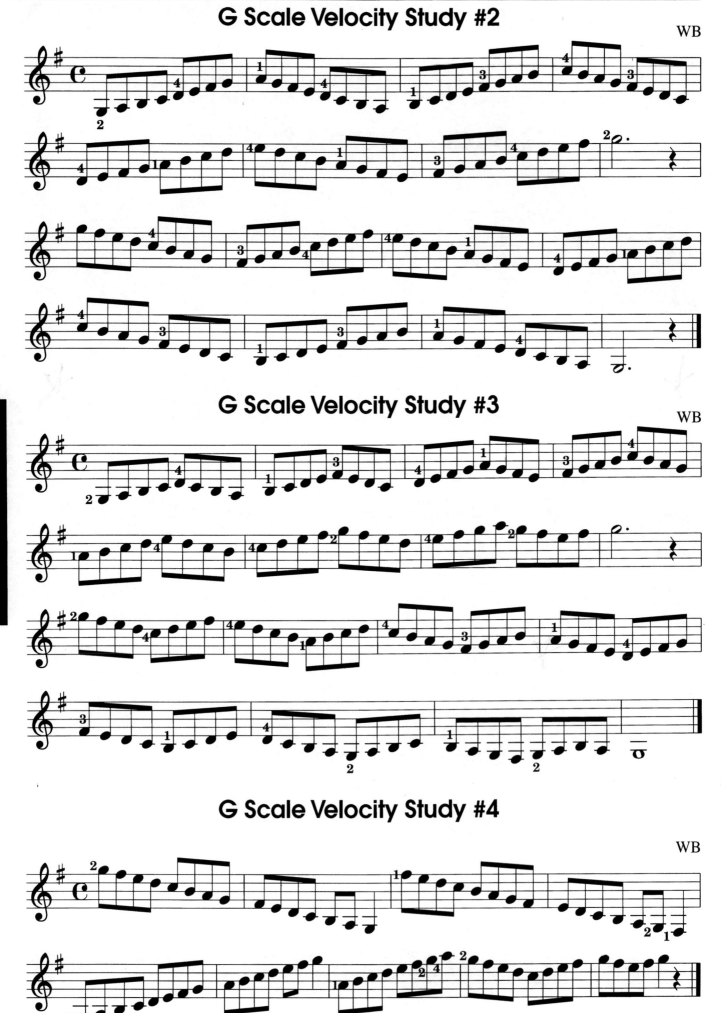

National Lancer's Hornpipe

Flatpick Solo
Lively ♩ = 160

CD #1 Track #36   WB

Witch of the Wave Reel

Flatpick Solo
Lively ♩ = 152

CD #1 Track #37   WB

Key of G

Days of ' Lang Syne

Flatpick Solo
Moderately ♩. = 50

CD #1 Track #38   WB
Scottish

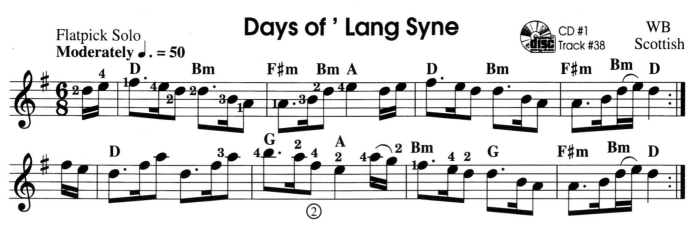

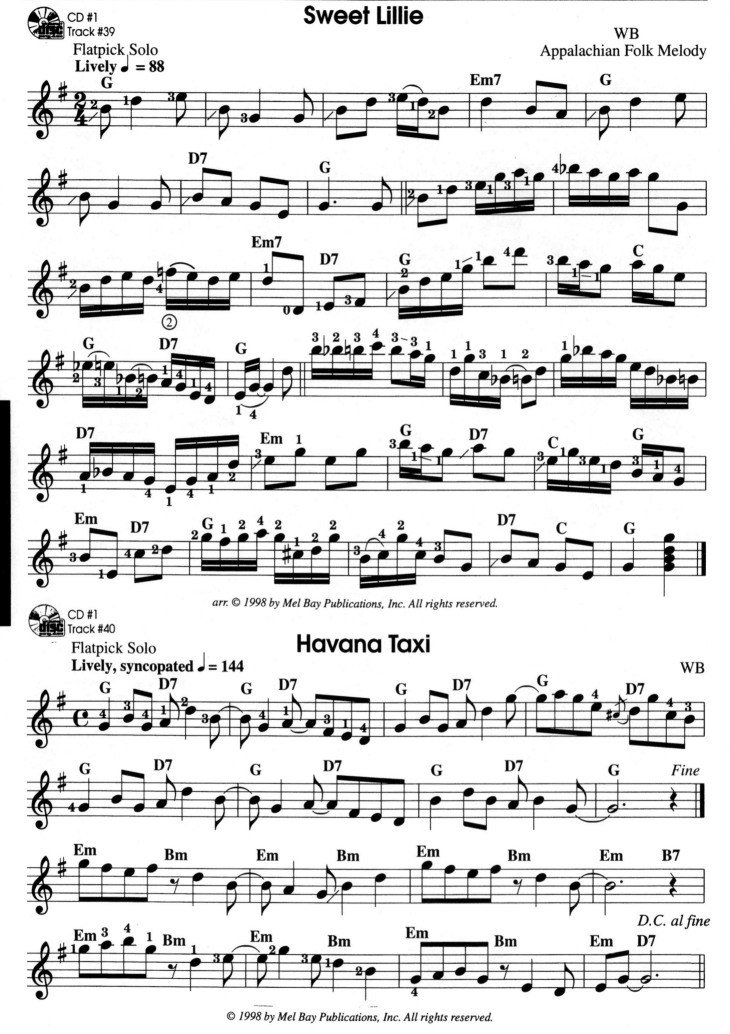

Bouree

WB
J.S. Bach

Flatpick Solo

* *tr* ~

Key of G

* Trill Top Note

Pretty Saro

CD #1
Track #42 American Ballad

WB

Key of G

$\frac{9}{8}$ Time

In $\frac{9}{8}$ Time there are nine beats to the measure. Each eighth note receives
one beat. The accents are on beats 1, 4, and 7.

Barney's Goat

CD #1
Track #43

WB
Irish Jig

Flatpick Solo

$\quad$ ♩. = 104

Silver Bell

CD #1
Track #44

WB
Fiddle Tune

Flatpick Solo
Swing feeling ♩ = 152

CD #1
Track #45

Miss McCloud's Reel

WB
Fiddle Tune

Flatpick Solo
Rousingly ♩ = 84

Key of G

CD #1
Track #46

Summer Serenade

WB

Tombigbee River

CD #1
Track #47

WB
Ballad

Prospect

CD #1
Track #48

WB
Early America
Hymn Tune

Key of G

Sinfonia

(From *Cantata #156*)

WB
J.S. Bach

Flatpick Solo

Adagio ♩ = 66

Key of G

Leather Britches

CD #1
Track #50

Flatpick Solo

WB
Fiddle Tune

Bop City

CD #1
Track #51

Flatpick Solo

WB

Key of G

Steep Canyon Rag

CD #1
Track #52

MC

Basic Improvisation in G
Basic Chords and Arpeggios in the Key of G

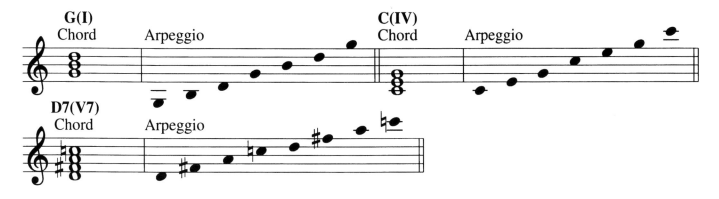

Play the following studies with a jazz or swing feeling.

Basic Arpeggios

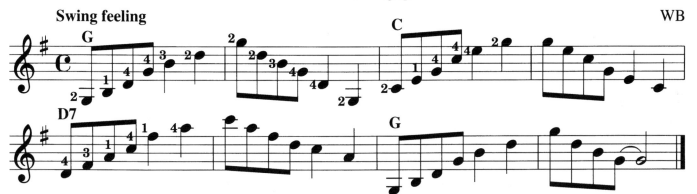

Passing Tone Arpeggio Study #1

Passing Tone Study #2

Chords/Arpeggios

Passing Tone Study #3

Rhythmic Variation Study #1

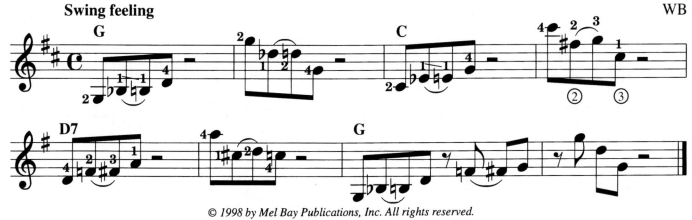

Rhythmic Variation Study #2

Rhythmic Variation Study #3

Make up your own rhythmic variation pieces!

Key of G

Jesu, Joy of Man's Desiring

CD #1
Track #53

WB
J.S. Bach

Flatpick Duet

Flowing ♩. = 66

Key of G

Key of G

Green Fields of America

CD #1
Track #54

Flatpick Solo
Lively ♩ = 88

WB

Gladiator Reel

CD #1
Track #55

With rhythm ♩ = 88

WB

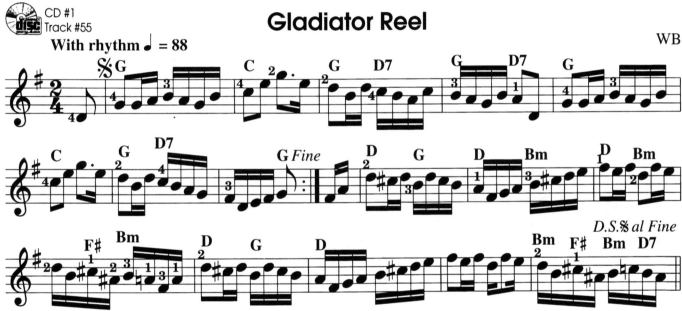

Key of G

Pacific Blues

CD #1
Track #56

Flatpick Solo
Slow groove ♩ = 120

WB

②

Menuett
(Duet)

CD #1
Track #57

MC
G.P. Telemann

Fingerstyle or Flatpick

Key of G

Groove Time

Flatpick Solo
Medium rock tempo ♩ = 120

CD #1
Track #58

WB

Breezin'

Flatpick Solo
Fast tempo ♩ = 132
Be-Bop feeling

CD #1
Track #59

WB

Riff for Clifford

Flatpick Solo
Very fast ♩ = 168
Be-Bop feeling

CD #1
Track #60

WB

Key of G

Theme for Bird

Flatpick Solo
Swing beat ♩ = 168
Be-Bop feeling

CD #1
Track #61

WB

Blue Vibes

Flatpick Solo
Medium tempo ♩ = 152
Jazz feeing

CD #1
Track #62

WB

"To Carlos"

Flatpick Solo
Medium ♩ = 152
Bossa Nova feeling

CD #1
Track #63

WB

Key of G

Black and White Rag

This is a famous fiddle contest rag. The first half is in the **key of G,** the second half is in the **key of C.** Notice that some passages are played in closed position. Some are in open position.

Chords in the Key of G

The chords in the **key of G** are drawn on the diagrams below. The basic chords are drawn first, followed by embellishments and alternate fingerings. The chords written at the top are chords in the key of G (these chords were presented earlier in this book).

G(I), C(IV), Am(ii), Em(vi) & Embellishments of G, C, Am, & Em

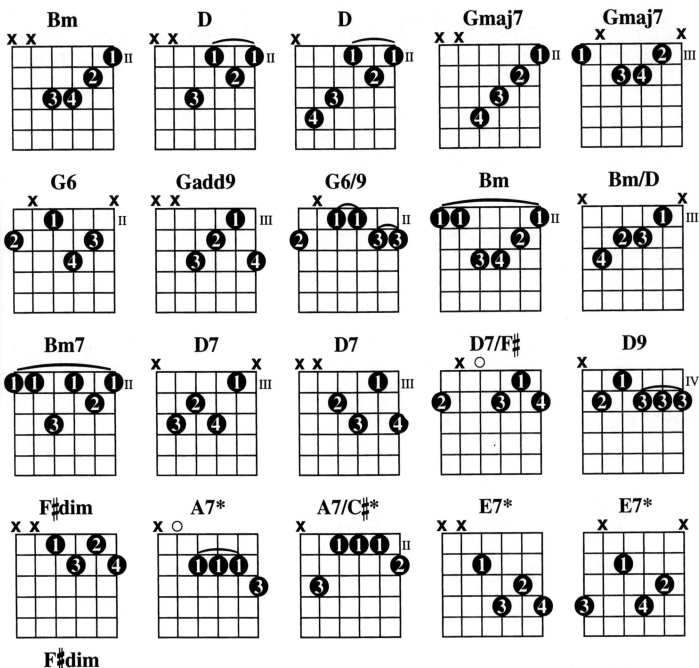

*These chords are not actually in the key of G, but they are commonly used when playing pieces in G.

Chord Progressions in G

Practice the following chord progressions using chords in the **key of G.** Use basic fingerings first, then try other fingerings. Use the strum or fingerpick pattern which is written in the first measure to play each measure of the exercise. You may also try other strum or fingerpick patterns.

Chord Studies in G

Little Chorale

Fingerstyle Etude

Play the following piece which uses chords written in note form.

Key of G

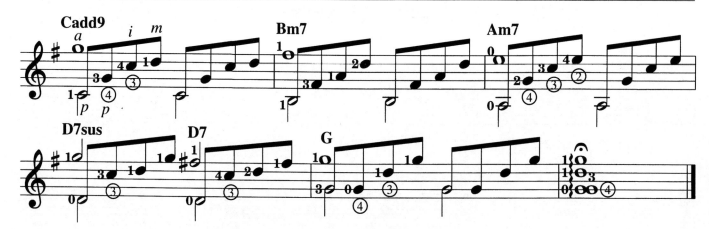

The following pieces are flatpick solos which contain arpeggios.

Spring Water

CD #1
Track #67
MC

Flatpick Solo
♩ = 96

Smooth Change

CD #1
Track #68
MC

Flatpick Solo
♩ = 76 Swing feeling

Key of G

CD #1
Track #69

Fifth Avenue Swing

Flatpick Solo
Slowly, easy swing

WB

Key of G

Easy swing

The following classical guitar solo shows how arpeggios may be found throughout a composition. Notice that this solo starts in the **key of G** and ends in **E minor**.

Op. 100 No. 2

CD #1
Track #70

MC
M. Giuliani

No Goodbyes

CD #1
Track #71

MC

Key of G

Blues in G

The following exercises are blues progressions in the **key of G.** In each measure use the strum or comp pattern which is written in the first measure. **Comp** is short for accompaniment. Comp patterns, commonly used in jazz, are usually short rhythm figures.

Turnarounds in G

Written below are some of the more common and popular turnarounds used for the **key of G.**

MC

Blues in the Key of G

The following solos contain turnarounds. The turnarounds have been boxed so they can be seen easily.

Mama's Blues

Flatpick Solo

MC

Blues in the Key of G

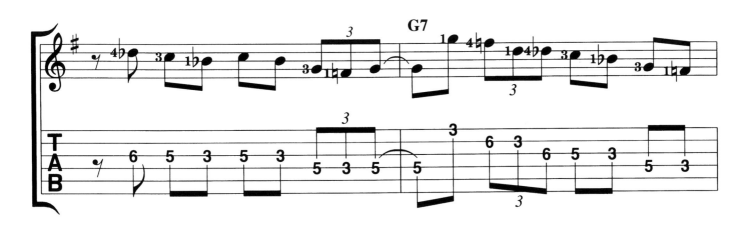

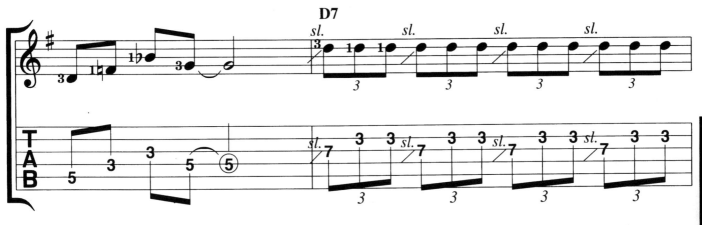

Blues in the Key of G

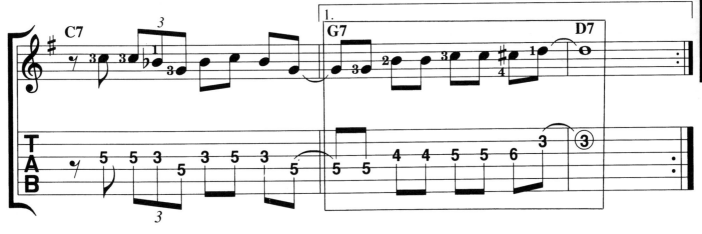

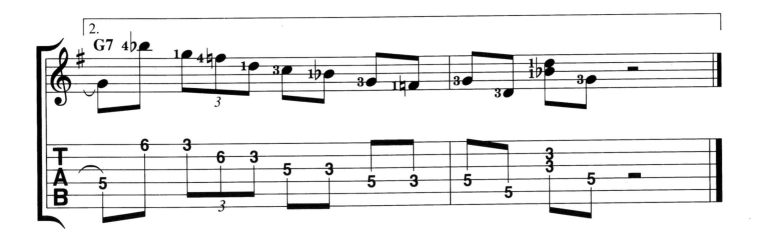

Gee Bop Blues

Licks/Fills/Breaks in G

Written below are some common licks, fills, and breaks used in the **key of G.** Practice the licks individually and then insert them into music in the key of G.

Licks/Fills/Breaks

The next solo in the key of G contains licks which have been boxed so they can be seen easily.

Good Times

Lick Variation

Principles of Memorization

By following a few simple guidelines, the process of memorizing music can be made much easier and the time it takes to do it can be greatly reduced. Many students think that the way to memorize music is to begin by playing it over and over. Actually, there should be several steps taken before the music is played. Begin by selecting music which is within reach. Don't try to memorize music which is so difficult it is way beyond your skill level. Also, always approach memorization with a feeling of confidence.

Before playing the music, scan it for directions (repeats), rhythm challenges, position shifts, fingerings, and the texture (single note, chords, music in two parts, etc.). Locate the difficult sections. There will probably be more time spent going over those areas when you begin playing. Before you begin playing, look over the music. Try to hear the rhythms and the basic direction of the pitch. Count and tap the rhythms without the guitar. Find the strong and weak beats. Sing the music out loud or silently while reading through it. Also, try to imagine fingering and playing the piece as you read through it.

Next, begin reading and playing the music. It's extremely important to the memorization process to play the piece correctly from the beginning. Use correct fingerings, rhythms, and pitches. If you change the music each time it is played, it will be much more difficult to commit it to memory. Be accurate from the beginning. Play the music as slowly as necessary to play it correctly.

It will be much easier to memorize the music if small sections are memorized one at a time, rather than playing the music over and over from beginning to end. See how much of the music can be handled at one time. Try for four-measure phrases. Play the section accurately several times. Eliminate the temptation to look at the music by turning it over. It may be helpful to sing the music while it is played. If there is hesitation or memory block, look at the music and repeat the process. It may be that a shorter span of the music will have to be attempted. At the first sign of error, stop, look at the music, and try again.

After memorizing one segment, move on to the next. Repeat the memorization process with the next short section of music. After each new segment is memorized, play the music from the beginning.

Don't be content with simply playing the correct notes and rhythms. Strive for smoothness and musicality while memorizing. Focus on tone, accents, and dynamics as well.

Minor Pentatonic Scale (Sixth-String Root)

Below is a diagram of a minor pentatonic scale. A pentatonic scale consists of five notes in one octave. This "scale pattern" may begin in any fret. The dot with the "R" pointing to it is the "root." The name of this note will determine the name of the scale. This pattern has the root of the scale on the sixth string.

The chart under the diagram shows the fret numbers and the names of the notes on the sixth string. If you play this scale pattern beginning in the fifth fret, it will be an A minor pentatonic scale because the sixth string, fifth fret, is an A. Practice this scale beginning on any fret. Play the notes in the order in which they're written in Exercise 1. Memorize this pattern.

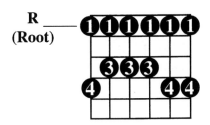

Fret	1	2	3	4	5	6	7	8	9	10	11	12
Root Name	F	F♯ G♭	G	G♯ A♭	A	A♯ B♭	B	C	C♯ D♭	D	D♯ E♭	E

Written above is the minor pentatonic scale beginning in the fifth fret, so it is an A minor pentatonic scale. If the scale had been written beginning on the sixth string, third fret, it would have been a G minor pentatonic scale because the note on the sixth string, third fret, is G.

It's **important,** after you practice the written solos in this section, that you create your own solos in **several different keys** using each scale. It would also be a good idea to transpose the written solos to different keys.

The following two solos use the F# minor pentatonic scale which has the root on the sixth string, second fret.

CD #1
Track #75

St. Louis Shuffle

Flatpick Solo

♩ = 96 (♫ = ♩♪)

MC

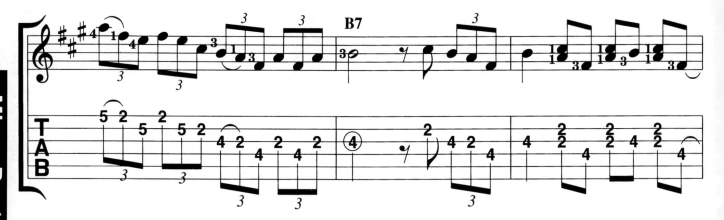

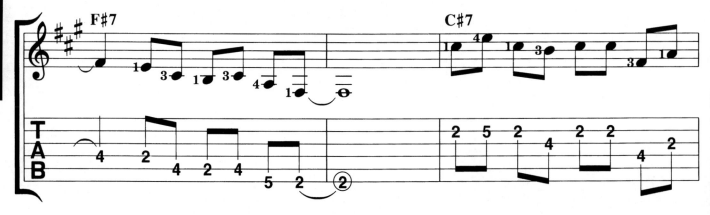

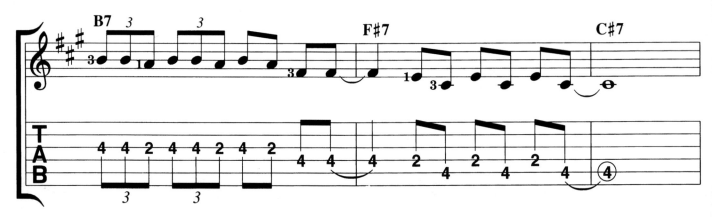

Minor Pentatonic Scale

Minor Pentatonic Scale

Midnight Stroll

CD #1
Track #76

Flatpick Solo

♩ = 84

MC

Minor Pentatonic Scale

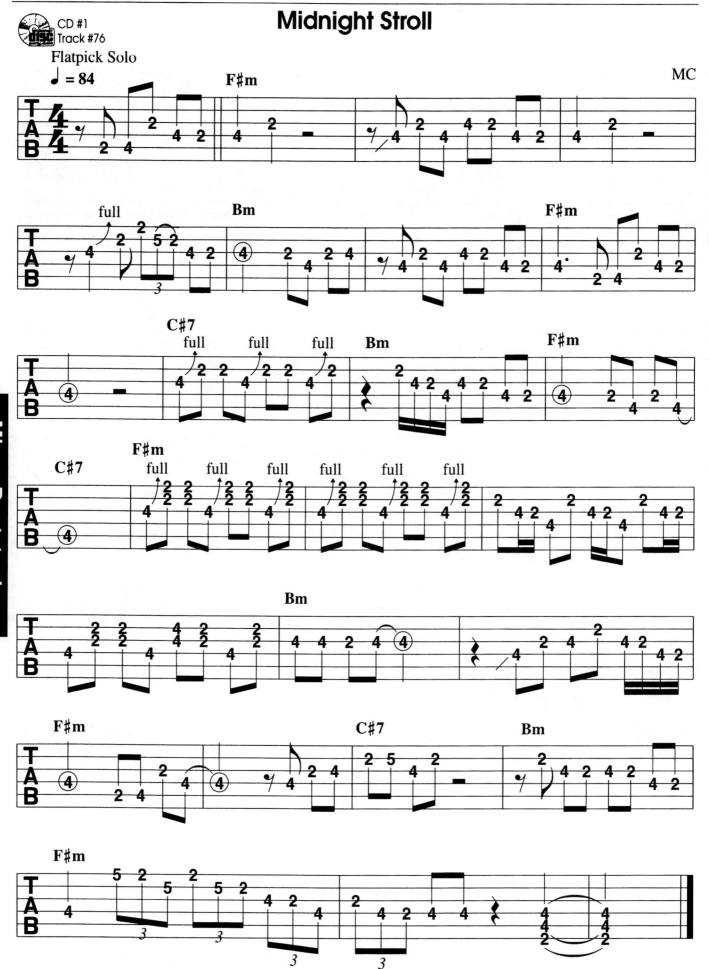

The next example shows how a solo can be transposed. This is the same piece ("Midnight Stroll") which was played in F#m, only now it is in Am. The solo has now been transposed to A minor. The notes which are used come from the A minor pentatonic scale which has the root on the sixth string, fifth fret. Notice the fingering is exactly the same as the solo in "Midnight Stroll" in F#m.

Midnight Stroll

Minor Pentatonic Scale

Minor Pentatonic Scale (Fifth-String Root)

The next diagram shows the **minor pentatonic scale** which has the root (the note which names the scale) on the fifth string. The chart above the diagram shows the names of the notes and their fret numbers on the fifth string. If you want to play a C minor pentatonic scale, you would position the pattern so the root is in the third fret on the fifth string. To play a D minor pentatonic scale, you put the root on the fifth fret, fifth string.

Fret	0	1	2	3	4	5	6	7	8	9	10	11	12
Root Name	A	B♭ A♯	B	C	C♯ D♭	D	D♯ E♭	E	F	F♯ G♭	G	G♯ A♭	A

Practice the following scale which is the **D minor pentatonic scale** with the root on the fifth string, fifth fret.

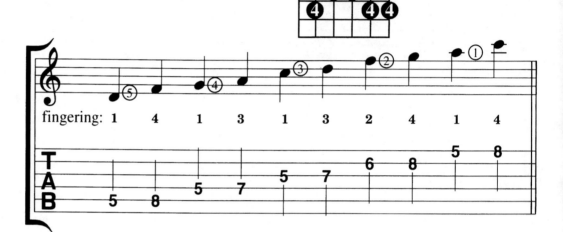

The following solo is a blues in the **key of B minor.** The notes used for the solo come from the B minor pentatonic scale with the root on the sixth string, second fret.

Drive Me Away

Flatpick Solo
♩ = 96

CD #1
Track #77

MC

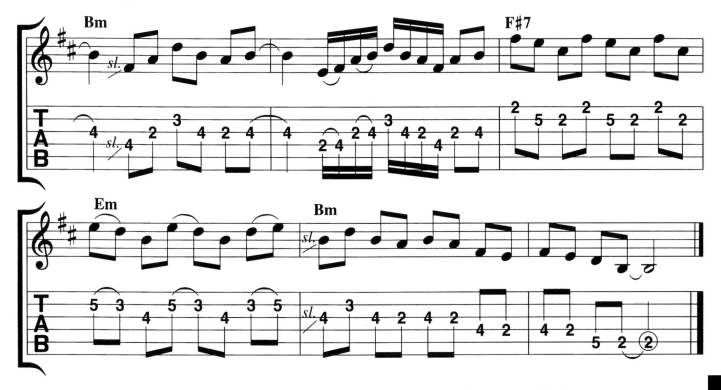

The next solo is in D minor. It uses the **D minor pentatonic scale** with the root on the fifth string, fifth fret.

Can't Do That

CD #1
Track #78

MC

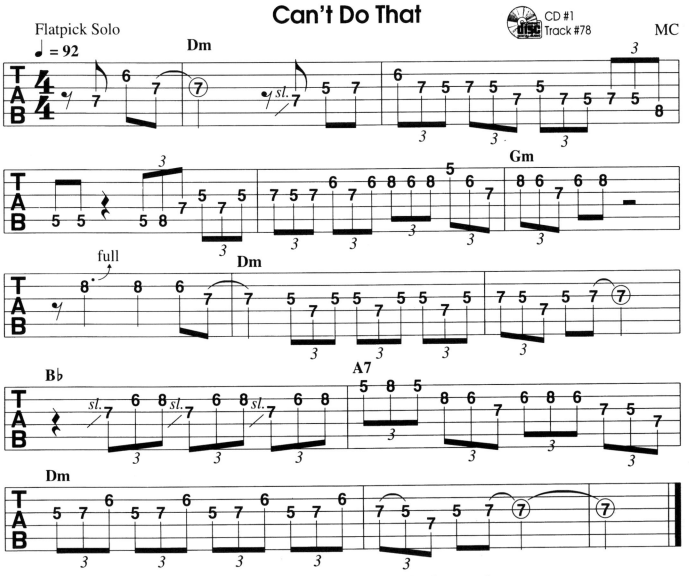

Key of D/Closed Position

We are now ready to learn the **key of D** in Zone 1/Closed Position. This form of the D scale lies in what has traditionally been called second position since the **first finger of the left hand** is on the **second fret.**

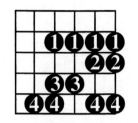

Velocity Study #1

WB

Velocity Study #2

WB

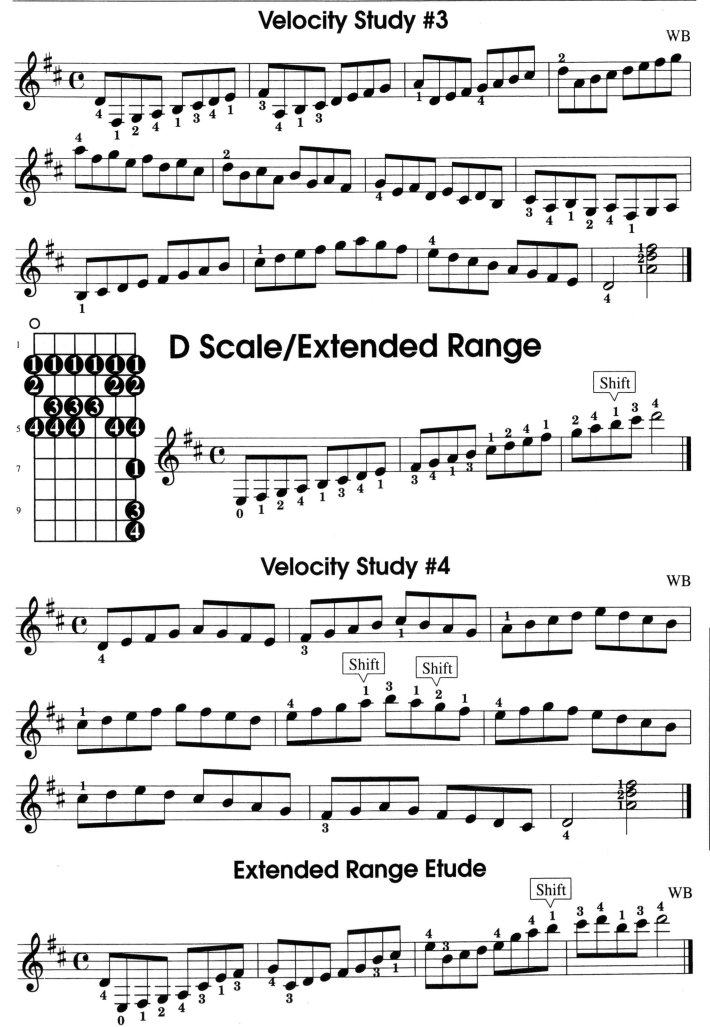

Velocity Study #3

D Scale/Extended Range

Velocity Study #4

Extended Range Etude

CD #1
Track #79

Bonaparte Crossing the Rhine

Flatpick Solo

WB
Fiddle Tune

Moderately ♩ = 88

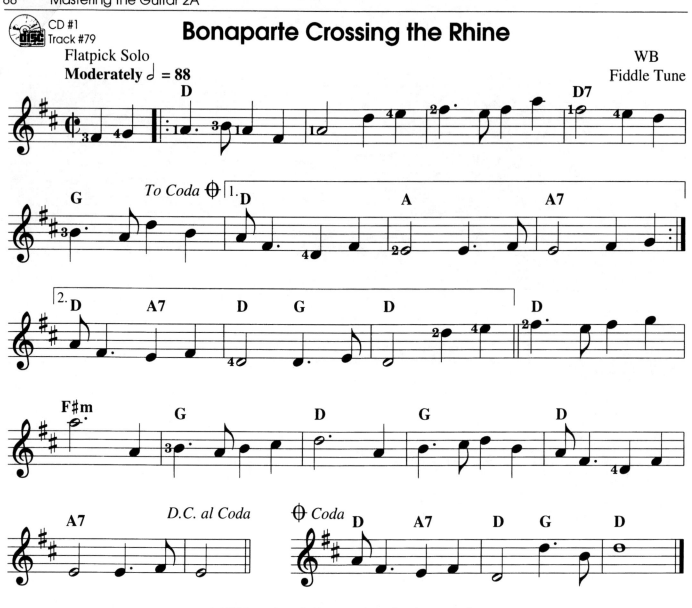

CD #1
Track #80

Back Manner Tune

Flatpick Solo

WB
Shaker Song

Rhythmically ♩ = 80

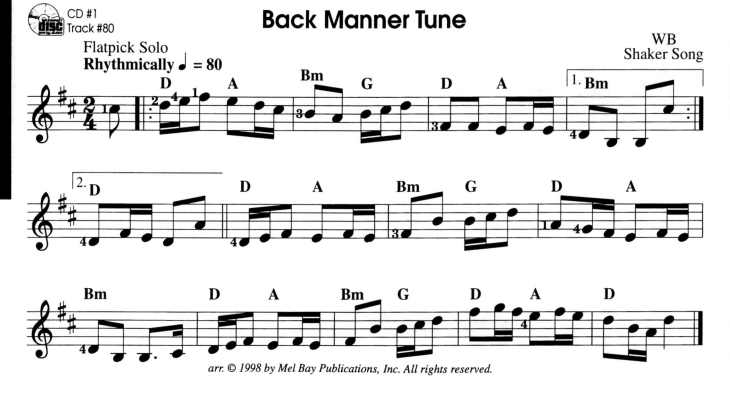

An Comhra Donn

Flatpick Solo

Lively ♩ = 144

WB
Hornpipe

St. Clair's Hornpipe

Flatpick Solo

Bright, lively dance feeling ♩ = 80

WB

Key of D

CD #1
Track #83

Goin' Home Blues

Flatpick Solo
Easy blues groove ♩ = 126

WB

CD #1
Track #84

Pepe's Visit

Flatpick Solo
Light rock rhythm ♩ = 138

WB

Key of D

Star of Bethlehem

CD #1
Track #85

Flatpick Solo
Moderately ♩ = 138

WB

CD #1
Track #86

Bennett's Favorite Reel

Flatpick Solo
Lively ♩ = 80

WB

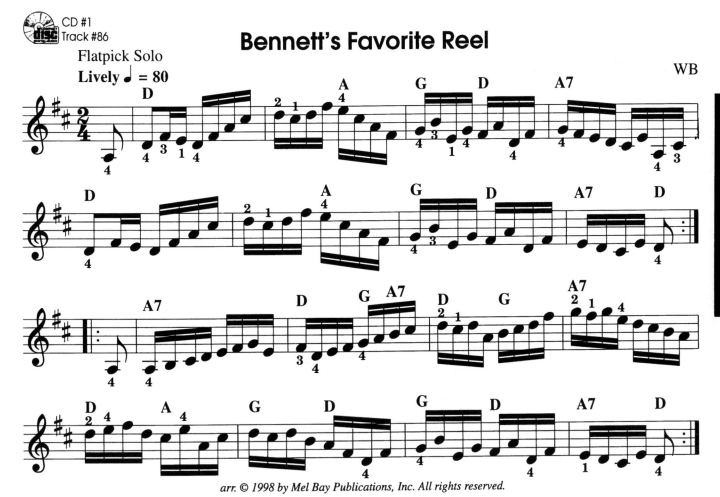

Key of D

CD #1
Track #87

Fugue in D

MC
Fernando Carulli

Flatpick or Fingerstyle Solo

♩ = 116

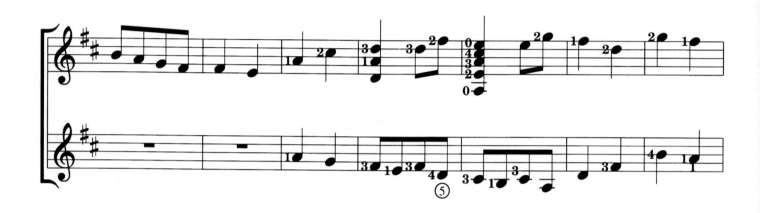

Key of D

CD #2
Track #1

Ivy Leaf Reel

Flatpick Solo

With spirit ♩ = 78

WB
Zeke Backus

CD #2
Track #2

St. Anne's Reel

Flatpick Solo

♩ = 84

WB

Key of D

Etude #11

Play with pick or fingers.

CD #2
Track #3

MC
Francisco Tarrega

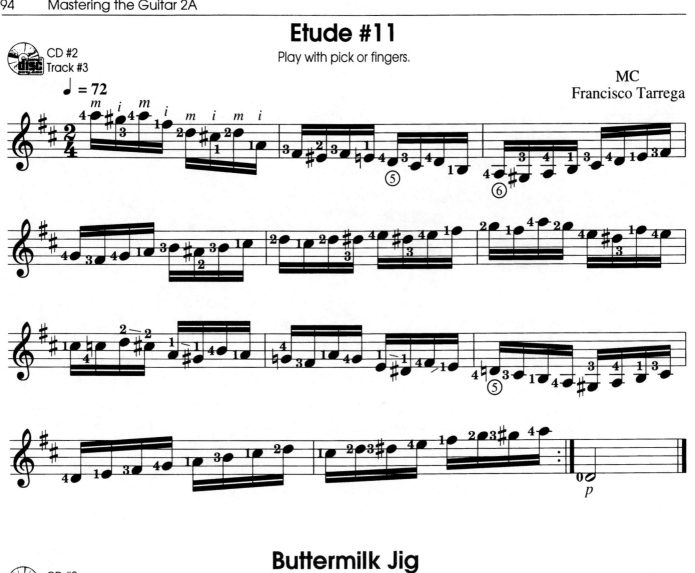

Buttermilk Jig

CD #2
Track #4

Flatpick Solo

Lively, with rhythm ♩. = 96

WB

Key of D

Neapolitan Threshers

Whiskey Before Breakfast

Sauget Strut

Key of D

Notes on the Second String

	B	C	C# or Db	D	D# or Eb	E	F	F# or Gb	G	G# or Ab	A	A# or Bb	B

Second String Study #1

Play all notes **only** on the second string

WB

Second String Study #2

Play all notes **only** on the first and second strings.

WB

Notes on the Second String

Basic Improvisation in D
Basic Chords and Arpeggios in D

Basic Arpeggios

Passing Tone Study #1

Passing Tone Study #2

Chords/Arpeggios

Passing Tone Study #3

Rhythmic Variation Study #1

Rhythmic Variation Study #2

Rhythmic Variation Study #3

Make up your own rhythmic variation pieces!

Key of D

Autumn
(Duet from *The Four Seasons*)

This famous piece is arranged as a guitar duet. Pay close attention to the frequent changes in dynamics from loud to soft and back to loud.

First Guitar – pick or fingers; standard tuning.
Second Guitar – pick or fingers; Dropped-D tuning.

CD #2
Track #8

WB
Vivaldi

Key of D

CD #2
Track #9

"D" Blues

Medium with solid beat ♩ = 108

WB

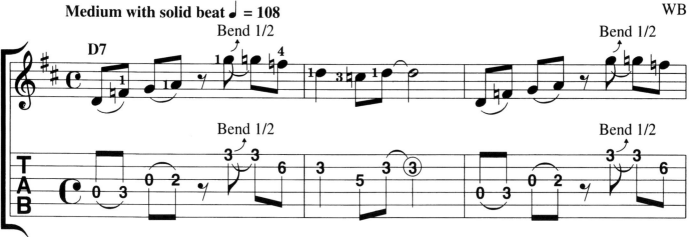

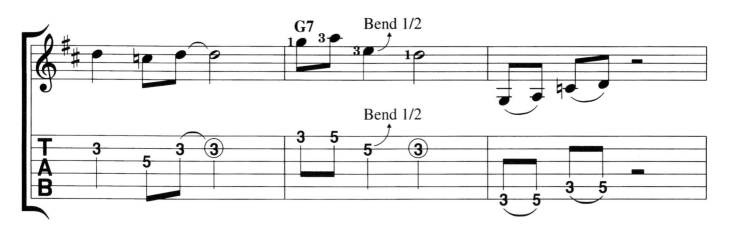

Key of D

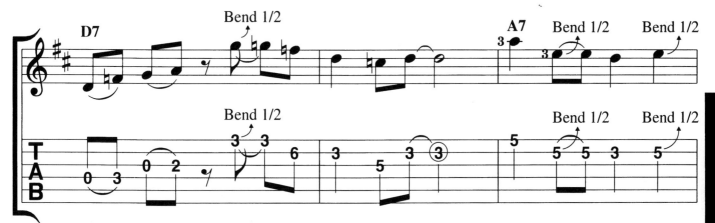

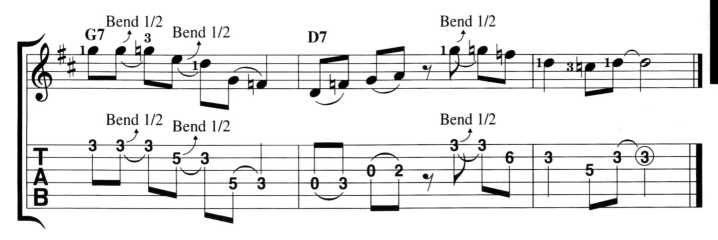

Hornpipe from 'Water Music'
(Theme/Duet)

CD #2
Track #10

3/2 Time   In **3/2** Time we have 3 beats per measure. Each half note receives one full beat.

The first part may be played with pick or fingers. The second part is to be played with fingers only.
The second guitar uses Dropped-D tuning.

WB
Handel

⑥ = D **Moderately** ♩ = 96

Key of D

Key of D

Notes on the Third String

G	G# or Ab	A	A# or Bb	B	C	C# or Db	D	D# or Eb	E	F	F# or Gb	G

Third String Study #1

Play all notes **only** on the third string

WB

Third String Study #2

In the following exercise, the top note is played on the first string. The second note from the top is played on the second string. The bottom note is played on the third string.

WB

Chords in the Key of D

Drawn below are the new chords in the **key of D**. The chords written on the top are in the key of D but have been presented earlier in this book. The basic chords are shown first, followed by the embellishments and optional fingerings.

D(I), Em(ii), G(IV), Bm(vi), & Embellishments of D, Em, G, & Bm

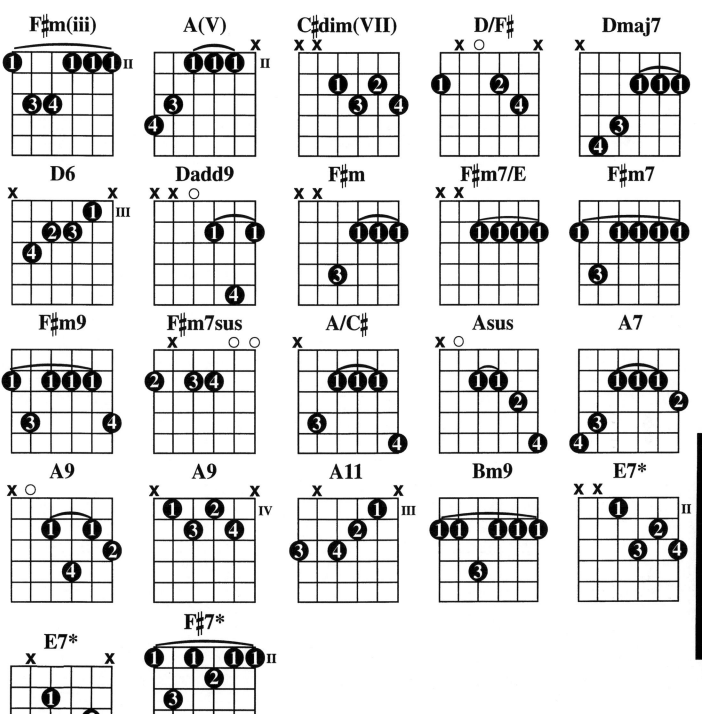

*These chords are not actually in the key of D, but they are frequently used when playing pieces in D.

Chord Exercises in D

Play the following exercises using chords from the **key of D.** At first, use the strum or fingerpick pattern which is written in the first measure to play each measure of the exercise. Then, you may want to try other patterns.

Chord Studies in D

The next solo uses arpeggios of some of the chords from the **key of D.**

Evening Shade

Chords in the Key of D

Meditation

Hazy Afternoon

Key of D

Mother Has Come With Her Beautiful Song

Fair Flower of Northumberland

Key of D

Swingin' on a Cloud

Flatpick or Fingerstyle Solo
Dropped-D Tuning

⑥ = D   **Easy, swing guitar feeling** ♩ = 72

CD #2
Track #16

WB

Key of D

Lovely Love

CD #2
Track #17

Flatpick Solo
Dropped-D Tuning

WB
Shaker Melody

Very slowly ♩ = 52

Key of D

Theme from 'Winter'

(Duet from *The Four Seasons*)

First Guitar – pick or fingers; Dropped-D tuning.
Second Guitar – fingerstyle; Dropped-D tuning.

WB
Antonio Vivaldi

CD #2
Track #18

⑥ = D   **Largo cantabile, very slowly** ♩ = 44

Key of D

Key of D

Notes on the Fourth String

| D | D# or Eb | E | F | F# or Gb | G | G# or Ab | A | A# or Bb | B | C | C# or Db | D |

Fourth String Study #1

Play all notes **only** on the fourth string

WB

D String Boogie

Play all notes on the fourth string.

WB

Notes on the
Third String

Arkansas Traveler

CD #2
Track #19

Fingerstyle Solo
Dropped-D Tuning

Moderatly fast ♩ = 63

arr. by Mel Bay
American Fiddle Tune

⑥ = D

molto ritard.

Key of D

Jock O' Hazeldean

Fingerstyle
Dropped-D Tuning
Slowly lyrically ♩ = 60

CD #2
Track #20   **WB**
Scottish Ballad

Key of D

Cottonwood Samba

CD #2
Track #21

MC

Fingerstyle Solo

Key of D

The following classical pieces are fingerstyle solos in the **key of D.**

Rondo

Fingerstyle Solo

Allegro ♩. = 63

CD #2
Track #22

WB
Fernando Sor

Saltarello

CD #2
Track #23

Fingerstyle Solo
Dropped-D Tuning

⑥ = D

MC
Vincenzo Galilei

Key of D

Key of D

CD #2
Track #24

Allegro

Fingerstyle

WB
Giuliani

Allegro ♩ = 120

p m a m i m a m
or p i m i p i m i

Key of D

CD #2
Track #25

Canary Jig

Fingerstyle Solo

♩ = 108

MC
Traditional

Key of D

Study in D

CD #2
Track #26

Fingerstyle Solo

Moderato ♩ = 72

WB
Sor

rit.   *a tempo*

Key of D

Gavotte I
(From *Cello Suite #6*)

CD #2
Track #27

Fingerstyle Solo
Moderately, gracefully ♩ = 88

WB
J.S. Bach

Key of D

Clair de Lune

This piece introduces new notes and some new time markings. Play it slowly and with expression. Play with pick or fingers.

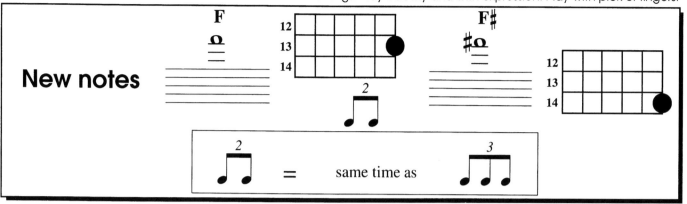

Key of D

Blues in D

The following progression is a 12-bar blues in the **key of D**. Use the same strum (comp) pattern which is written in the first measure to play each measure. You may also want to try using other strum patterns.

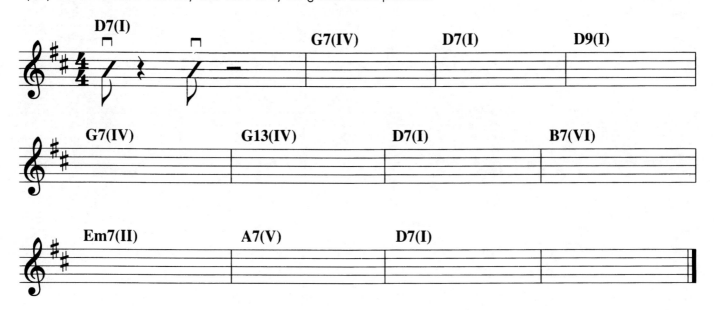

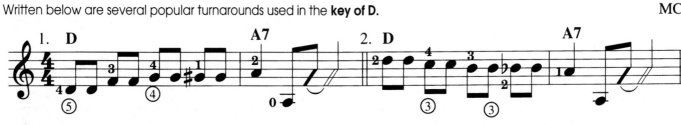

Turnarounds in D

Written below are several popular turnarounds used in the **key of D**.

MC

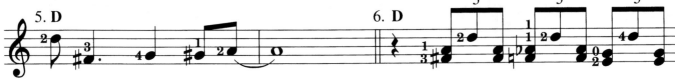

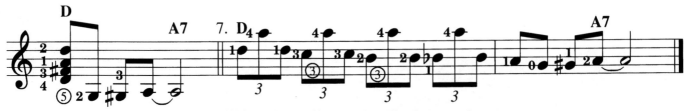

"Atlantic Blues" is a solo containing turnarounds in the **key of D.** The turnarounds have been boxed.

Flatpick Solo

Atlantic Blues

CD #2
Track #29

MC

Blues in the Key of D

Licks/Fills/Breaks in D

Written below are some of the common licks, fills, and breaks used in the **key of D.** Practice them separately and then insert them into music you play in the key of D.

Licks/Fills/Breaks

The next solo contains some licks in D. So they can be seen easily, the licks have been boxed.

Louisiana Connection

Flatpick Solo

♩ = 152 (♩♩ = ♩♩♩)

MC

Licks/Fills/Breaks

Principles of Successful Performance

The key to a successful performance can be summarized in three words...preparation, preparation, and preparation! Preparation creates confidence. Confidence helps create a successful performance. Inadequate preparation leaves the performer unsure about the next move and uncomfortable with the performance situation. The preparation for the performance begins with practicing properly. Practice sessions (especially those just before the performance) should be approached as though they are mini-performances. Certain techniques which can be used in practicing will help make the final performance a positive experience.

After you can play the piece, practice trying to see and hear ahead as you play. After notes have been played, they are no longer important. Don't dwell on them. If you should make a mistake, it's history...block it out and forget it. If you should miss a note, going back and trying to correct it will break the continuity and flow of the music. Continue playing as though nothing had gone wrong. The average listener may not notice the wrong note, but most everyone notices a break in the rhythm.

Do not make false starts. If you should make a mistake, don't go back and pick up the pieces. Starting over highlights the mistake. Hear the piece before you begin to play, and imagine yourself playing the piece well. Set the tempo in your mind before you begin playing.

Practice with the performance as the goal. Constantly imagine yourself playing the music in front of a audience. Be aware of how you look. Do you look pleasant and like you're enjoying the moment? The mood of many of the listeners will depend upon how you look and conduct yourself. It's okay to smile and move with the music. Have a positive attitude toward your listeners. Be glad they came to listen.

Thinking about making mistakes, about the audience focusing on you, about being nervous, and about the quality of your playing are some common negative thoughts which will cause nervousness.

Don't communicate negative feelings to the audience. While it may be difficult to eliminate all of these feelings from the performance, try to replace negative feelings with positive ones. To eliminate negative feelings, focus on the music and playing it well. Let the audience see and hear that you are confident and comfortable with the music. Let them share your enthusiasm and enjoyment.

A certain amount of nervousness is to be expected and can actually help make a better performance. Learn to accept and deal with your nervousness.

One key ingredient which will be of great help in preparing for a successful performance is a series of practice, or mini, performances. First, do a performance alone. Concentrate on playing the music correctly (i.e. proper notes, fingerings, etc.). Do this type of a performance several times...each time in a new location. Don't hesitate in the music and don't stop. Before the performance, check the tuning and sing (in your mind) the first portion of the music. Breathe deeply several times before you begin playing.

Next, do a performance for one or two people. Practice entering and bowing as though it were the final performance.

After performing for one or two people, play for a small audience. This could be for friends or other students. At this time concentrate on putting expression into the piece. It may be a good idea to play the music a bit slower than normal for this performance. Ignore errors.

Finally, do the final performance for a larger and more general audience. By this time you have created enough confidence to be able to enjoy the experience. Tell yourself, "the hard part is over." Remember, it is very important to focus positively on your playing and have a positive attitude toward the performance and the listeners.

Successful Performances

Moveable Power Chords

The following diagram shows a power chord which may be moved up or down the neck. The note with the "R" pointing to it is the "root." The name of this note will be the name of the power chord. The circle is an optional note. It is the octave and can be added to the chord or left off. The loop under the diagram indicates only strings six and five are to be played. Remember to play only those strings which have fingers on them.

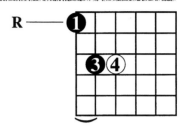

The following chart shows the names of the roots on the sixth string and the fret numbers in which they are played:

0	1	3	5	7	8	10	12	-	fret
E	F	G	A	B	C	D	E	-	root name

Power chords may be played on any step of the scale. For example, B5 would have the root in the 7th fret:

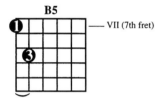

To sharp a power chord, move it up one fret; to flat a power chord, move it down one fret.

Practice the following exercises using power chords with the root on the sixth string. Use only downstrokes.

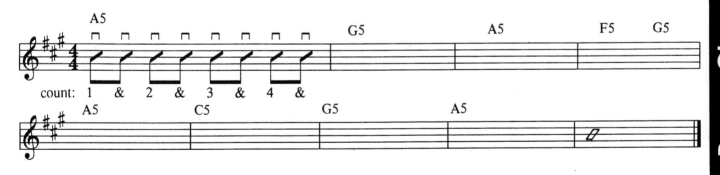

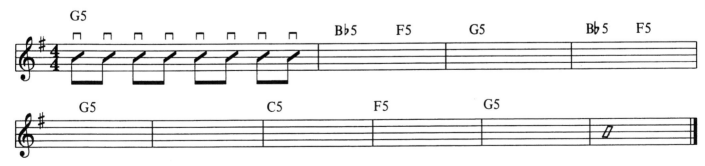

Power Chords

A power chord may also have its root on the fifth string. The following diagram shows the fingering for this group of power chords. Remember, the circle is an optional finger.

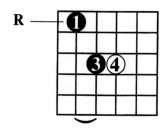

The following chart shows the fret numbers for the root names on the fifth string:

0	2	3	5	7	8	10	12	-	fret
A	B	C	D	E	F	G	A	-	root name

Drawn below are two examples of power chords with their roots on the fifth string:

As with the other power chords, sharp the chord by moving the pattern up one fret, and flat the chord by moving it down one fret.

Practice the following progressions using power chords with roots on the fifth string.

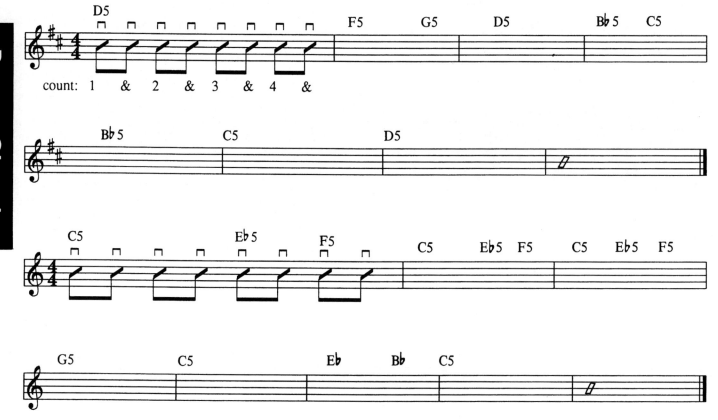

By combining power chords with the roots on the sixth string with power chords having roots on the fifth string, it is possible to change chords and keep them close to each other. Practice the following exercises using both groups of chords. In the first exercise, the chords with the roots on the sixth string are indicated with "R/6," and the chords with the roots on the fifth string are indicated with "R/5." On the other exercises, you decide which power chord to use. Try to keep the patterns close to one another. On the first exercise below, play eight downstrokes in a measure. On the other exercises, play the rhythms which are written in the measures. Use only downstrokes.

Rock Comping

A very popular technique used in rock guitar rhythm playing is to use broken rhythms. This is a type of "comping," which is short for accompaniment. The following patterns can be used to play songs in 4/4. They are very popular in rock and funk styles. Each pattern takes one to two measures to complete. The same pattern can be used throughout the song, or more than one pattern can be used.

Hold any chord and practice the following patterns. Barre chords and power chords may sound the best with these exercises. Be careful to count the rhythm and watch the strum direction.

Practice the following progressions. In each exercise continue playing the pattern which is written in the first one or two measures. The numbers in parentheses show which pattern is being used.

Repeat the pattern written in the previous two measures.

The following exercises show how several of these comp rhythms can be combined.

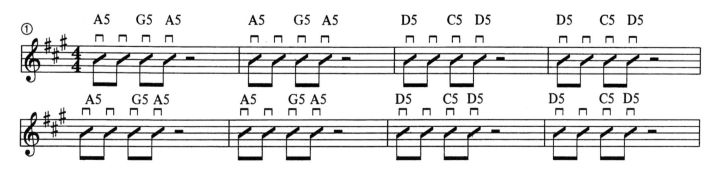

Play the following progressions using your own combinations of the comping rhythms. Also, try to create some of your own rhythms.

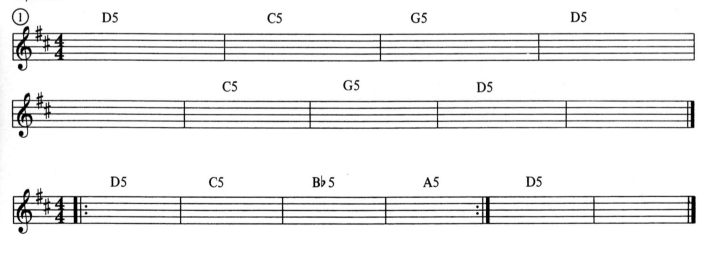

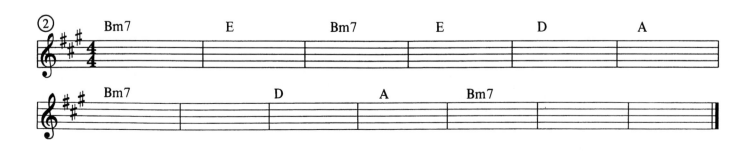

$\frac{12}{8}$ Time

In 12/8 time there are twelve counts in a measure and the eighth note gets one count. When counting 12/8 time, rather than counting all twelve beats, it's common to divide the twelve beats into four groups of three beats as shown below. Each measure would then be counted as though it contained four beats.

Time values in 12/8 for the various kinds of notes and rests are shown below.

o·	= 12 beats	♩·	= 3 beats	▬	= 8-12 beats
o	= 8 beats	♩	= 2 beats	▬	= 4 beats
♩·	= 6 beats	♪	= 1 beat	𝄽·	= 3 beats
♩	= 4 beats	♬	= 1/2 beat	𝄽	= 2 beats
				♪	= 1 beat
				♪	= 1/2 beat

Practice "She's Gone Away," which is a solo in 12/8 time.

She's Gone Away

Key of B Minor

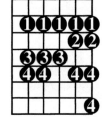

The key of B minor has two sharps, F♯ and C♯.

The Natural B Minor Scale

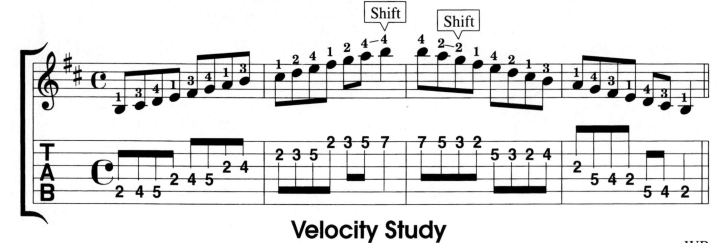

Velocity Study

WB

The B Harmonic Minor Scale

Velocity Study

WB

Key of B Minor

Harvest Moon Strathspey

Flatpick Solo
Moderately ♩ = 112

CD #2
Track #32

WB

Brighton Beach

Flatpick Solo
Spirited tempo ♩ = 108

CD #2
Track #33

WB

Low Rider

Flatpick Solo
Rhythmically ♩ = 66

CD #2
Track #34

WB

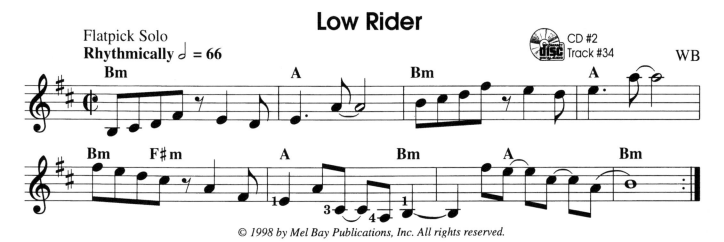

Caliente

Flatpick Solo
Latin Rhythm ♩ = 144

CD #2
Track #35

WB

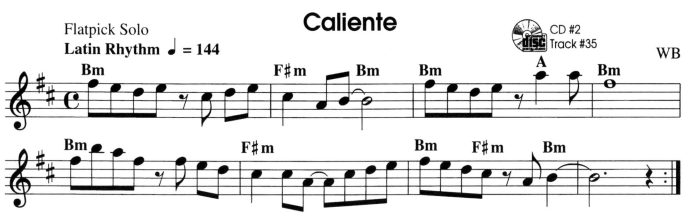

Key of B Minor

Alastair's Lament

Flatpick Solo
Slow, march-like tempo ♩ = 126

CD #2
Track #36

WB

Avenging and Bright

CD #2
Track #37

WB
Thomas Moore

Flatpick Solo
Slow, free tempo, expressive ♩ = 96

Luckie Bawdins' Reel

CD #2
Track #38

WB
Scottish

Flatpick Solo
Rhythmically ♩ = 112

Key of B Minor

Deco Dance

CD #2
Track #39

Flatpick Solo
Swing jazz feeling ♩ = 126

WB

Last Tango in Skokie

CD #2
Track #40

Flatpick Solo
Tango Rhythm ♩ = 116

WB

D.C. al Fine

Key of B Minor

North Sea

Flatpick Solo
Moderately ♩. = 100

CD #2
Track #41

WB

Puttin' on the Glitz

Flatpick Solo
Fast swing tempo ♩ = 132

CD #2
Track #42

WB

Key of B Minor

Etude

CD #2
Track #43

WB
Clodmir

Flatpick Solo
Moderately ♩ = 66

Soaring

CD #2
Track #44

Flatpick Solo

MC

Key of B Minor

CD #2
Track #45

Marziale

Flatpick Solo

Moderately, expressively ♩ = 60

WB
St. Jacome

Key of B Minor

Notes on the Fifth String

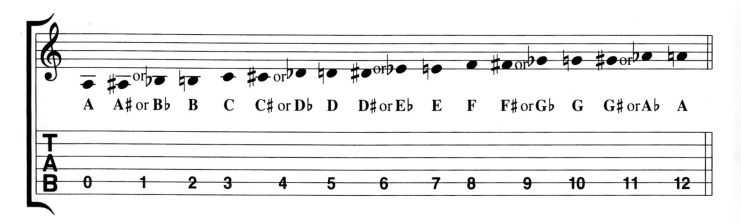

A	A# or Bb	B	C	C# or Db	D	D# or Eb	E	F	F# or Gb	G	G# or Ab	A

"A" Drive

Play all the notes on the A string.

WB

"A" Boogie

Play all notes on the fifth string.

WB

Moderately

C

Notes on the
Fifth String

B Minor Swing

Flatpick Solo

CD #2
Track #46

MC

© 1998 by Mel Bay Publications, Inc. All rights reserved.

Remembrance

Flatpick Solo
Slowly, with feeling ♩. = 60

CD #2
Track #47

WB

© 1998 by Mel Bay Publications, Inc. All rights reserved.

Luna Noche

Flatpick Solo
Moderately ♩ = 138

CD #2
Track #48

WB

© 1998 by Mel Bay Publications, Inc. All rights reserved.

Key of B Minor

Basic Improvisation in Bm

Basic Chords and Arpeggios in Bm

Basic Chords and Arpeggios in Bm

Basic Arpeggios

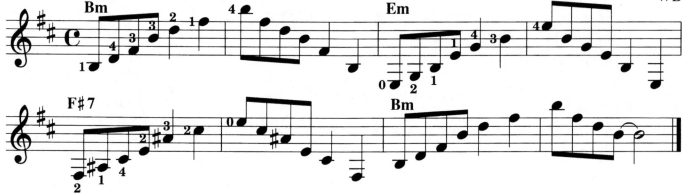

Passing Tone Study #1

Passing Tone Study #2

Chords/Arpeggios

Passing Tone Study #3

WB

Rhythmic Variation Study #1

WB

Rhythmic Variation Study #2

WB

Rhythmic Variation Study #3

WB

Make up your own rhythmic variation pieces!

Chords/Arpeggios

Preludio

First Guitar – play with pick or fingers. **Second Guitar** – play fingerstyle
Second Guitar – tune sixth string down to D.

CD #2
Track #49

WB
Corelli

Key of B Minor

Key of B Minor

Jezebel Carol

CD #2
Track #50

WB
Carol from the
Isle of Man

Flatpick Solo

Slow ♩ = 72

CD #2
Track #51

Noël Nouvelet

WB
French carol

Flatpick Solo

Slowly ♩ = 76

HoldChord

Key of B Minor

Minuet

Northumbrian Dance

Key of B Minor

Hired Hands

CD #2
Track #54

MC

Notes on the Sixth String

E   F   F♯ or G♭   G   G♯ or A♭   A   A♯ or B♭   B   C   C♯ or D♭   D   D♯ or E♭   E

0   1   2   3   4   5   6   7   8   9   10   11   12

Walkin' Jazz

Play all notes on the sixth string.

WB

Funky Sixth

Play all notes on the sixth string.

WB

Medium tempo

Notes on the Sixth String

CD #2
Track #55

Bouree

(From *Suite #2*)

First Part – fingerstyle or flatpick. **Second Part** – fingerstyle.

Allegro ♩ = 84

Embarcadero

Bright, rhythmic tempo ♩ = 132

WB

Key of B Minor

Chords in the key of B Minor

Drawn below are the new chords in the **key of B minor.** The chords written on the top are also in the key of B minor but have been presented earlier in this book. The basic chords in the key are shown first followed by the embellishments and optional fingerings.

Bm(i), D(iii), Em(iv), G(VI) & Embellishments of Bm, D, Em & G

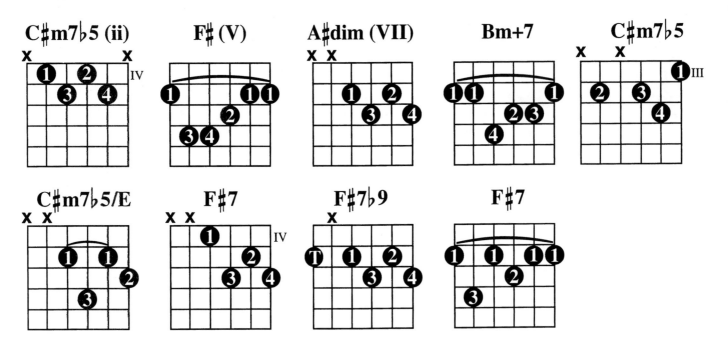

Practice the following chord progressions which use chords from the key of B minor. In each measure of the exercise, play the comp, strum, or fingerpick pattern which is written in the first one or two measures.

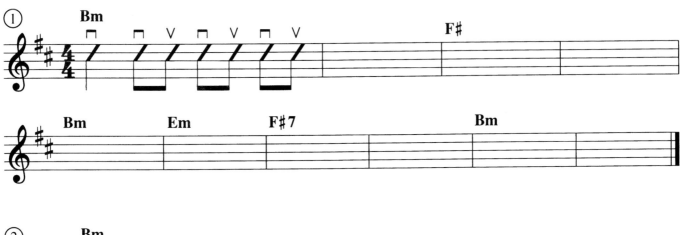

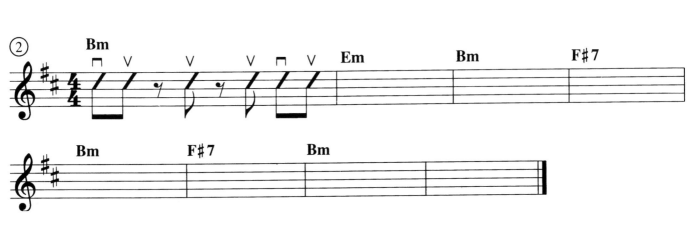

③

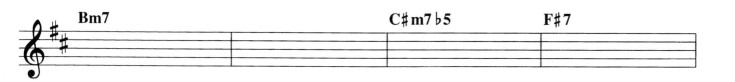

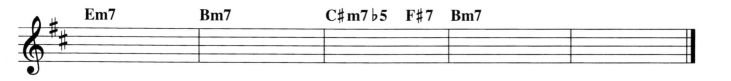

④

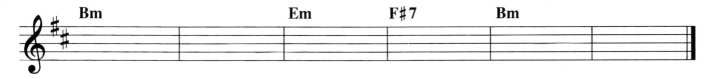

⑤

Chords in the Key of Bm

⑥ Bm7   C♯m7♭5 F♯7   Bm7   C♯m7♭5 F♯7

Em7   Bm7   F♯7   A♯dim   Bm7

⑦ Bm   Em   Bm

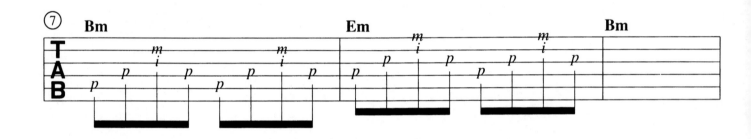

F♯7   Gmaj7   F♯7   Bm

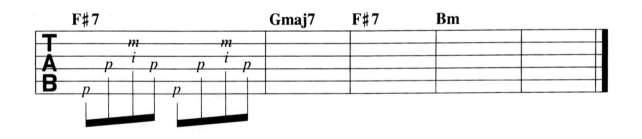

⑧ Bm   Bm+7   Bm7   Bm+7

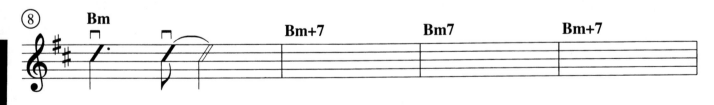

Bm   F♯7♭9   Bm

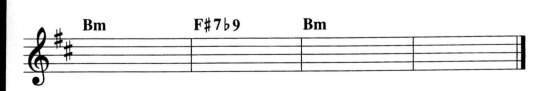

Chord Studies in B Minor

CD #2
Track #57

Flatpick Solo

B Minor Etude #1

MC

♩ = 114

Chords in the Key of Bm

B Minor Etude #2

CD #2
Track #58

MC

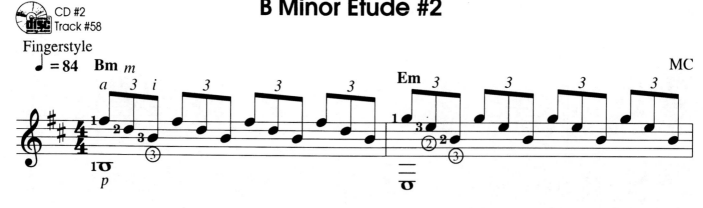

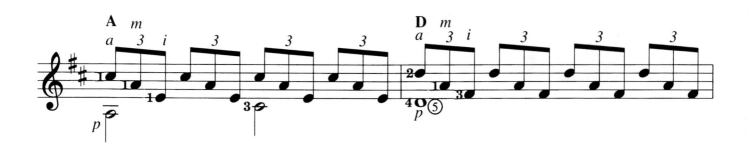

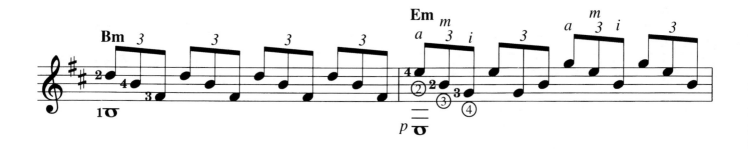

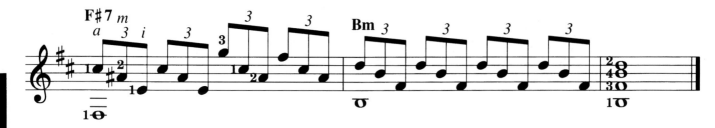

Key of B Minor

El Brujo

CD #2
Track #59

WB

Bad Vibes

CD #2
Track #60

WB

Key of B Minor

Key of B Minor

The next solo, "Romance of Spain," is an arpeggio study. To play the piece smoothly, figure out all of the notes in one or two measures...hold those notes and then begin playing. Let all the notes ring.

Romance of Spain

CD #2
Track #63

Key of B Minor

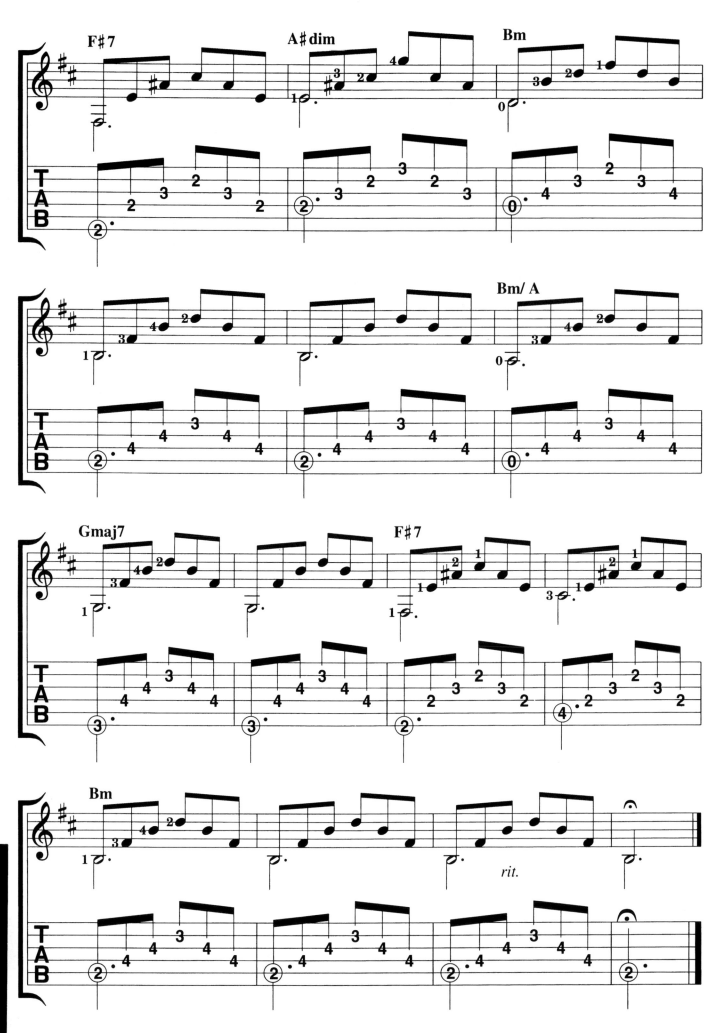

Jungle Fever

CD #2
Track #64

Flatpick Solo

♩ = 112

MC

Key of B Minor

CD #2
Track #65

Visions of Madrid

MC

Strum the chord in this measure

Key of B Minor

B Minor Waltz

Key of B Minor

Etude

Fingerstyle
Moderato ♩ = 104

CD #2
Track #67

Sor

Study in Bm

CD #2
Track #68

Fingerstyle
Allegretto ♩ = 76

Sor

Key of B Minor

Prelude

CD #2
Track #69

Sor

Key of B Minor

D.C. al Fine

Key of B Minor

Blues in B minor

Written below are two twelve-bar blues progressions in the **key of B minor.** Use the same strum pattern which is written in the first measure of the exercise. You may also want to try using other strum patterns.

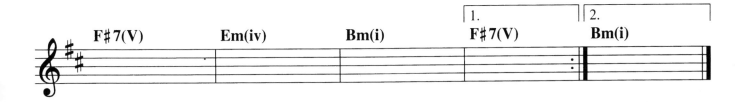

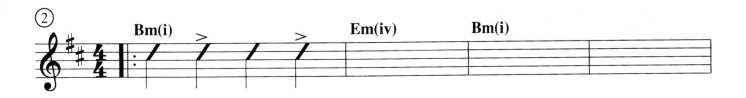

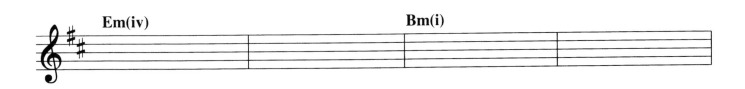

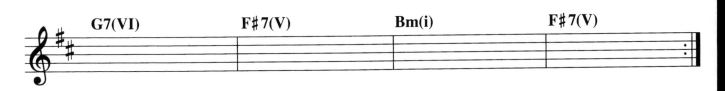

Blues in B minor

"Got the Time" is a blues solo in **B minor.** Play it up to tempo and use swing rhythm.

CD #2
Track #70

Got the Time

Flatpick Solo

MC

Blues in B minor

Licks/Fills/Breaks in B minor

Written below are some of the common licks, fills, and breaks used in the key of B minor. Practice them separately and then insert them into music you play in the **key of B minor.**

Licks/Fills/Breaks

The next solo contains some licks in **B minor.** So they can be seen easily, the licks have been boxed.

Somethin' for Nothin'

Licks/Fills/Breaks

You are now ready to proceed to Mastering the Guitar Book 2B.

Licks/Fills/Breaks